CONSTELLATIONS

Like the future itself, the imaginative possibilities of science fiction are limitless. And the very development of cinema is inextricably linked to the genre, which, from the earliest depictions of space travel and the robots of silent cinema to the immersive 3D wonders of contemporary blockbusters, has continually pushed at the boundaries. **Constellations** provides a unique opportunity for writers to share their passion for science fiction cinema in a book-length format, each title devoted to a significant film from the genre. Writers place their chosen film in a variety of contexts – generic, institutional, social, historical – enabling **Constellations** to map the terrain of science fiction cinema from the past to the present... and the future.

'This stunning, sharp series of books fills a real need for authoritative, compact studies of key science fiction films. Written in a direct and accessible style by some of the top critics in the field, brilliantly designed, lavishly illustrated and set in a very modern typeface that really shows off the text to best advantage, the volumes in the **Constellations** series promise to set the standard for SF film studies in the 21st century.'
Wheeler Winston Dixon, Ryan Professor of Film Studies, University of Nebraska

 Constellations

@Constelbooks

T0311108

Also available in this series

Blade Runner Sean Redmond

Close Encounters of the Third Kind Jon Towlson

The Damned Nick Riddle

RoboCop Omar Ahmed

Rollerball Andrew Nette

Forthcoming

12 Monkeys Susanne Kord

Children of Men Dan Dinello

Dune Christian McCrea

Jurassic Park Paul Bullock

Mad Max Martyn Conterio

CONSTELLATIONS

Inception

David Carter

David Carter is retired Professor of Communicative English at Yonsei University, Seoul, and is now a freelance writer and translator. He formerly lectured on the history of German Cinema at Southampton University, UK, and has published books on *East Asian Cinema* (2007) and *The Western* (2008), and articles on German Expressionist Films and Film Remakes.

Acknowledgements
Special thanks are due to David Burton, a keen film enthusiast, who suggested several interesting lines of interpretation.

Dedication
For David, Ginette, William and Rebecca Burton, a family of film lovers.

First published in 2019 by
Auteur, 24 Hartwell Crescent, Leighton Buzzard LU7 1NP
www.auteur.co.uk
Copyright © Auteur 2019

Series design: Nikki Hamlett at Cassels Design
Set by Cassels Design www.casselsdesign.co.uk
Printed and bound in Great Britain

British Library Cataloguing-in-Publication Data
A catalogue record for this book is available from the British Library

ISBN paperback: 978-1-911325-05-5
ISBN ebook: 978-1-911325-06-2

Contents

I. Introductory Remarks

Inception is a difficult film to categorise. It partakes of various genres, blurring the distinctions between them. Yes, it is science fiction but it does not contain many of the ingredients associated with that genre. It can also be identified as a kind of heist film, and the first part of the film, the extraction, certainly involves a complex robbery; but then the second part of the film, while having many of the trappings of a heist, involves putting something *into* a heavily guarded location rather than stealing *from* it. There are shades of film noir as well, not only because of the heist motifs but also due to its character types. It can also be described as a psychological thriller, telling the story of one man's attempt to flee his past and regain access to his family, of his coming to terms with the death of his wife. In addition it plays with time, questioning the certainty of consciously experienced real time, and revealing that the personal experience of the passing of time is variable. The film also explores the nature of the mind and how dreams are related to the conscious and unconscious mind.

The first section of the book explores the director Christopher Nolan's biography and the themes of his other films, from early shorts to *Dunkirk* (2017). Then there is a brief account of how *Inception* was developed from its existence as a treatment, through production to its premiere. The problems of defining the film as belonging to a specific genre are explored at some length, with comparisons to other films sharing some characteristics with it.

As dreams feature so prominently in the film, several sections are devoted to related aspects of the film. First, some reflections on the oneiric theory of dreams are provided, and then Nolan'a own thoughts about the relationships between dreaming and filming and the challenges of depicting dream states in films are explored. To aid understanding of the structure and conventions in the film, examples of how the film uses specific aspects of dream theory are examined.

This study then focuses on the psychological and moral development of the main character, Cobb, and shows how he progresses from being defensive about his obsession with unresolved guilt problems concerning the circumstances of his wife's death to being able to confront these issues and overcome them, thus releasing him to return to a close relationship with his family.

Certain aspects of the visual arts, as exemplified in the work of M. C. Escher and Francis Bacon feature significantly in the film. Their general significance and roles in the film are examined.

Finally the much discussed ambiguous ending of the film is considered, including some reflection on how it might be interpreted.

For the purposes of further discussion some examples of the critical reception, both positive and negative, are provided, and suggestions are made for further lines of investigation of other aspects of the film which could not be explored in this short study.

Synopsis

The first part of the film depicts an attempt by Cobb (Leonardo DiCaprio) and his partners at extraction: a process which involves accessing the mind of the industrialist Saito (Ken Watanabe) via his dreams, to obtain secret information on behalf of another corporation. After the attempt fails, Saito is however sufficiently impressed by Cobb's techniques to ask him to perform inception on one of his business rivals: this involves planting an idea in the mind of the company's heir, Robert Fischer (Cillian Murphy), which will induce him to break up the business empire after his father's death. Cobb agrees to do this when Saito promises that he will make it possible for Cobb to return to his family in America. Cobb was forced to flee abroad to avoid arrest for the presumed murder of his wife, Mal (Marion Cotillard). The figure of Mal haunts Cobb's subconscious and hinders him and his partners in the inception process, which involves creating three dream levels, each within the other. Despite the baleful influence of Mal and the subconscious defence mechanisms within the mind of the subject, Fischer, inception is finally accomplished, and Saito ensures that Cobb can rejoin his children.

2. Christopher Nolan: The Director and His Work

The brief biography below provides only an outline of Christopher Nolan's life so far. No extensive biography of him has been published at the time of going to press. The basic facts have been gleaned from various articles about him and his films, from interviews with him, and from reliable websites. The films he has made are referred to only briefly in the context of the development of his career. More details on them are provided in the subsequent section on themes and ideas in his films. Sources consulted have been listed in the general bibliography. Other significant references are included in the endnotes.

Biography

Christopher Jonathan James Nolan was born on July 30, 1970, in London. His father, Brendan Nolan, was British of Irish descent, and was an advertising copywriter. His American mother, Christina (née Jensen), worked as a flight attendant. He was raised in both London and Chicago and has dual British and American citizenship. He has an older brother, Matthew, and a younger one, Jonathan, who has worked with him on many of his films. Jonathan writes for American television and has co-written screenplays with Christopher. It is known that Christopher Nolan had already become interested in making films by the age of seven. His father owned a Super 8 camera and allowed him to make short films with it, using toy action figures.

He was educated at the Haileybury and Imperial Service College, an independent school at Hertford Heath, Hertfordshire, England. He later studied English literature at University College, London (UCL). He has said that he chose UCL as a place to study, because he had heard about its film-making facilities. At the time it possessed 16 mm cameras and a Steenbeck flatbed editing suite. This editing equipment had become standard throughout the world because it could be used with both 16mm and 35mm optical and magnetic sound film. Nolan became president of the University Union Film Society, and together with his then girlfriend, Emma Thomas (later his wife and co-producer in the production company Syncopy, run by them), he planned the film society's programme of major 35 mm films. He used the money earned to produce his own 16 mm films during the vacations.

One of the early films he made while at UCL, together with a childhood friend Roko Belic, was *Tarantella* (1989). For this film he used the Super 8 format. It was broadcast on *Image Union*, a programme devoted to independent films and videos on the Public Broadcasting Service (PBS) in America. In 1995 he made *Larceny*, filmed over one weekend in black and white, which was shown at the Cambridge Film festival in 1996.

After he graduated Nolan directed some corporate videos and industrial films. And in 1997 he made the short film *Doodlebug*. He developed many ideas for film projects during this period but was not able persuade anyone in the British film industry to finance them. 1998 saw the release of his first full-length feature film, *Following*, which he financed himself, with a budget of £3,000. It was made at weekends over a period of one year. In order not to waste precious film stock, each scene was rehearsed extensively, to ensure that no more than one or two takes of each shot would be necessary. It was co-produced with Emma Thomas, and Nolan did all the filming and editing himself. It won considerable critical acclaim.

As a result of the success of *Following*, Nolan was able to attract interest in another project he had been working on since 1997. He developed the screenplay based on an idea for a short story that his brother Jonathan was writing under the title *Memento Mori*. An executive with Newmarket films, Aaron Ryder, was impressed by the project and awarded him a budget of $4.5 million dollars. The film now titled *Memento*, premiered in September, 2000, at the Venice International Film Festival. It not only received great critical acclaim but was also a box-office success and received several awards and award nominations.

The success of *Memento* led to Nolan being offered the chance by Steven Soderbergh to direct the film *Imsomnia*, a remake of the Norwegian film of the same name of 1997. This film was also well-received by critics and was a box-office success. After *Imsomnia* Nolan worked on several projects which were not produced. He had written a screenplay about the filmmaker, business tycoon and inventor, Howard Hughes, but gave up the project when he heard that Martin Scorsese was making a film on the subject (*The Aviator*, 2004). He also worked on an adaptation of Ruth Rendell's novel *The Keys to the Street*, but eventually withdrew from this too because it bore too many similarities to films he had made already. Then in 2003 he approached Warner Bros. with the idea of making a new Batman film, which would have greater dramatic and psychological depth than the comic-book versions already made (*Batman Begins*, 2005). Following this he produced, directed and co-wrote with his brother an adaptation of the novel *The Prestige*, by Christopher Priest, released in 2006. In July of that year Nolan announced that he would be making a sequel to *Batman Begins*, to be called *The Dark Knight*, which was released in 2008. It was to be deeper and broader in scope than any previous 'superhero' films, and was nominated for eight Oscars at the 81st Academy Awards, winning the award for Best Sound Editing and a posthumous award for Heath Ledger as Best Supporting Actor.

Nolan now went on to write, direct and co-produce the film *Inception* for Warner Bros. which was released on July 16, 2010. It was nominated for eight Oscars, including that for Best Picture. It won Oscars for Best Cinematography, Best Sound Mixing, Best Sound Editing and Best Visual Effects. It was also nominated for BAFTA, Golden Globe, DGA and PGA awards.

Although he was at first hesitant about doing yet another Batman sequel he agreed to make a third and final Batman film in 2012. He developed a screenplay together with his brother Jonathan and David S. Goyer. *The Dark Knight Rises* was released on July 20, 2012. It proved to be as successful as its two predecessors. It will always be remembered, however, for a tragic event associated with it, which gave rise also to several copy-cat events. On the evening of the film's release, a mass shooting occurred in the Century Movie Theater in Aurora, Colorado, during a midnight screening of the film. A man, dressed in combat gear, set off tear gas grenades and shot into the audience with several firearms, killing 12 people and wounding 70 others. The perpetrator, James Eagan Holmes, was arrested shortly after. The event had an immediate effect on the publicity for the film. Warner Bros. cancelled gala premieres in Mexico, Paris and Japan, as well as some television commercials for the film. The production company made a substantial donation to help the victims of the shooting. Christopher Nolan also expressed condolences on behalf of both cast and crew. Measures were taken in many cities to avoid any copy-cat incidents. Several hoaxes and scares occurred but none caused fatalities.

Nolan's subsequent involvement in productions in the capacities only of producer and related executive roles has not guaranteed the critical success of the films in question. Such was the case with *Man of Steel* (2013), directed by Zack Snyder, which was an updated version of the Superman story, and *Transcendence* (2014), directed by the cinematographer Wally Pfister, who had worked on all of the films directed by Nolan since *Memento*.

Nolan was director, writer and producer on *Interstellar*, released on November 7, 2014. It is a science-fiction story of a space journey, based on ideas developed by his brother Jonathan, and utilising theories of the theoretical physicist Kip Thorne, who was scientific consultant for the film. His latest film at the time of writing is *Dunkirk*, which was released in July, 2017. The script, also by Nolan, related the events of the Allied retreat from Dunkirk in May, 1940.

Themes and Ideas in Nolan's Films

From his earliest short films (*Tarantella*, and *Larceny*),it is clear that Nolan has been interested in strange states of mind, illusions of various kinds, and the borderlines between fantasy and reality. Even his first experiments with his father's Super 8 camera were made using toy action figures. In *Doodlebug* (1997), we see a man on his hands and knees, holding a shoe by the toe and trying to kill some sort of insect, which constantly evades him. When he eventually manages to kill it he discovers, on looking at it closely, that it is a miniature version of himself. Whatever interpretation might be made of the film, one aspect of it is undeniable: it has a dreamlike quality. Having accepted the reality of the situation (a man chasing an insect), the audience is suddenly confronted with a bizarre and disturbing fact, and then the film ends, i.e. the audience 'wakes up'.

Following (1998)

Jeremy Theobald, *Following*

Nolan's first full-length feature film, *Following* was inspired by his experiences living in London and also by having his flat burgled. On the alumni page of the UCL website Nolan is quoted as saying, with reference to this film: 'There is an interesting connection between a stranger going through your possessions and the concept of following people at random through a crowd – both take you beyond the boundaries of ordinary social relations.'[1] The film tells of a young man who is unemployed but fancies himself as a writer and decides to follow people chosen randomly as they go about their lives, in the hope that this will provide him with some inspiration. He admits at one point in the film that things started to go wrong when his choice of person ceased being random. He becomes obsessed with one young man, to whom he finally speaks. This man, who identifies himself as Cobb (the same name that Nolan was to use later for the main character in *Inception*), reveals that he is a burglar, but one who is not interested in material gain. He burgles for the sake of the adrenalin it stimulates. He is interested in people and their relationships to their possessions ('You take it away, show them what they had'). Under Cobb's guidance the young man attempts burglaries himself. The plot then becomes very complex, and its complexity is made more difficult to comprehend by Nolan's adoption of a non-linear narrative structure. It is not necessary to unravel the plot in the present context, but there are various twists which reveal Cobb to be an ingenious manipulator. The non-linear narrative structure of the film is so complex that it is difficult for the viewers to reconstruct in their minds the precise temporal sequence of events. At a later stage in the film there are sequences which must clearly have occurred prior to ones already seen, and it is easy to wrongly identify some locations. Nolan has explained his decision to structure his film in this way in an interview: 'In a compelling story of this genre we are continually being asked to rethink our assessment of the relationship between the various characters, and I decided to structure my story in such a way as to emphasise the audience's understanding of each new scene as it is first presented.'[2] This pressure on the audience to understand 'each new scene as it is first presented' is maintained in his subsequent films. By the time he made *Inception* he was forcing his audience to understand not only the actual temporal sequence of juxtaposed events but also various events occurring contemporaneously but at different speeds (at different dream levels) and, further, to identify whether any given sequence was in the 'real' (diegetic) world as presented in the film or in one of the dream worlds.

Memento (2000)

In *Memento*, Nolan explored the relationship between memory and identity, which is a theme taken up again in *Inception*. The central character in *Memento*, Leonard, suffers from what is medically termed 'anterograde amnesia': 'a condition in which events that occurred after the onset of the amnesia cannot be recalled and new memories cannot be formed.'[3] Leonard knows that his wife was killed and he tries to track down the killer and take his revenge. Because of his mental condition, he can only retain memories of recent events and people for a very short period of time, after which they are obliterated. In order to cope with this condition he writes many notes to himself to remind himself of important facts and he also has information tattooed on his body. Leonard experiences his condition very much as if it were a dream: he finds himself suddenly in the present, in a situation, but does not know how he came to be there. This is because he has no short-term memory of what has

Guy Pearce, *Memento*

happened prior to that situation. Leonard describes it as follows: 'It's like waking. It's like you just woke up.' As with dreams, one cannot recall how one got into a dream but only how one came out of it. The man who is apparently trying to help him, Teddy, reinforces this at one point: 'You're living in a dream, kid.' His condition also entails a loss of a sense of the passage of time. Lying in bed Leonard asks, 'How am I supposed to heal if I can't feel time.' This loss of short-term memory and the sense of time does not, however, affect Leonard's awareness of his own identity, because he still possesses his long-term memory of events and information acquired before the incident which caused the amnesia. It does make him sensitive to the fact, however, that our sense of our own identity is closely tied up with our memories: 'We all need memories to remind ourselves who we are.'

As with *Following* Nolan plays with the time sequence again. He decided to use a narrative structure for *Memento* which would enable the audience to identify with Leonard's state of mind. And, again, Nolan constructed the narrative so that the audience would have to understand 'each new scene as it is first presented'. Some scenes are in colour and others are in black and white. The colour sequences tell the story in reverse order, and the black and white ones reflect Leonard's thoughts in monologue. In the documentary material on the second DVD disk included in the box-set of the film, there is a sequence entitled 'Anatomy of a Scene', in which it is explained that the director decided to help the audience cope with this complexity by providing clues in the title sequence. He provides hints, as it were, that they should expect to experience the passage of time in an unconventional way. Actions in the title sequence are run backwards: a Polaroid photograph 'undevelops' and bullets roll backwards and 'leap' upwards, etc. In telling his story in reverse Nolan is careful not to reveal too much, which might destroy the suspense about what really happened, but to help the audience piece it together there is duplication of the final sequence of each colour scene at the beginning of the scene which would, in correct time sequence, follow it. The audience thus finds itself suddenly in a scene which feels familiar, without being sure how it is connected to what went before: very much like Leonard himself. The colour thus also emphasises the vividness of experiencing the present moment.

Insomnia (2002)

The next film which Nolan made was not so experimental in terms of its narrative structure, but reveals a continuing preoccupation with themes explored in the earlier films. *Insomnia* (2002), was a remake of the 1997 Norwegian film of the same name directed by Erik Skjoldbjærg. Nolan's film is about two Los Angeles detectives sent to a northern Alaskan town to investigate the murder of a local teenage girl. The town is so far north that, as in the original Norwegian film, the leading detective finds it difficult to cope with the 'white nights', the summer nights when the sun never sets and there is constant daylight. It aggravates his insomniac condition. There is thus also throughout the film a suspension of the sense of the normal passage of time, as usually marked by the cycle of day and night. As a result of his condition, the detective, Will Dormer (played by Al Pacino) has hallucinations occasionally of his colleague, whose death he has on his conscience: he shot him while pursuing another man in a landscape covered with thick fog. It is unclear whether the killing was accidental or deliberate. For reasons which need not be explained in detail here, Dormer has a strong motivation for wanting the colleague dead and knows that he will not be believed if he reports the death as an accident caused by himself.

Al Pacino, *Insomnia*

The young local police officer, Ellie Burr (Hilary Swank), investigates the shooting and discovers a discrepancy between the type of bullet casing found at the scene of the shooting and the type believed to have been found in the body. She starts to suspect that Dormer is covering up the true circumstances for some reason. Dormer's prime suspect in the girl's death, Walter Finch, a local writer (played by Robin Williams), clearly has his own suspicions about Dormer and taunts him. The film provides a compelling investigation of the nature of conscience, the effects of guilt, and the complexities of human motivations and actions. The twists and turns of the plot need not concern us in the present context, but relevant to a consideration of Nolan's interests and preoccupations is Dormer's state of mind. With his sense of time confused, and at times hallucinating, Dormer cannot on occasions tell what is real and what is imagined. Nor can he tell sometimes whether he remembers something correctly or whether he only imagines that he does. Finch taunts him on the phone: 'Are you seeing things yet?' There is one sequence in the film which is truly like a nightmare: Dormer chases Finch over a river full of floating logs and falls between them into the water. For some time he is trapped beneath them, struggling to get back to the surface. Some parallels can be drawn between the use of the bullet casing as a motif in the last scene of the film and the spinning top token in *Inception*, which is used in the later film to distinguish between dream-world and reality. For

Burr to throw the bullet casing away would allow Dormer to maintain his fiction intact, but Dormer warns her 'Don't lose your way', and she retains the bullet casing as evidence of what really happened.

Some reflections on relevant aspects of the three films of the Batman trilogy made by Nolan will be included subsequently in consideration of all three films together, but it is worth paying particular attention first to a film he made between the first and second of the Batman films: *The Prestige*.

The Prestige (2006)

Hugh Jackman and Andy Serkis, *The Prestige*

Nolan co-wrote, directed and produced this adaptation of the novel of the same name by Christopher Priest, published in 1995. The film, as the novel, tells of the rivalry of two magicians in London at the end of the 19th century. Each tries to outdo the other in perfecting the most remarkable magic trick. One of them, Alfred Borden (Christian Bale), is sentenced to death for the murder of the other, Robert Angier (Hugh Jackman), by drowning him in a tank of water during Angier's own performance. The film relates in retrospect the complex series of events that led up to Borden being imprisoned, and then at the end there are a number of unexpected twists. To recount more details of the plot here would spoil enjoyment of the film for those who have not seen it. In an interview with *Variety* Nolan has mentioned that a special challenge in adapting the novel into a film was how to interpret the literary devices of the novel in cinematic terms, specifically 'the shifting points of view, the idea of journals within journals and stories within stories'.[4] This challenge is not far removed from that of presenting dreams within dreams in *Inception*. A common Nolan theme which features in the film is the frequent difficulty of distinguishing between illusion and reality. When an illusion cannot be explained, then the effect must be real. In an argument with Angier, his *ingénieur*, John Cutter (Michael Caine) exclaims 'It has no trick, it's real!' And the effects produced in the film by the scientist Nikola Tesla (played by David Bowie), a real historical figure, and which depend on the use of electricity, are real and not based on cleverly devised illusions. In one of the unexpected twists revealed at the end of the film, it turns out that Borden's wife has been living an illusion: her marriage has been not at all what she believed it to be. And both in the case of the old Chinese magician in the film and in that of Borden the success of a brilliant magic trick depends on living an illusion in real life, so that no one can ever suspect the truth.

Three concepts are introduced in the film, which denote the different stages of a magic trick. They can also be applied to the structure of the film as a whole, and, incidentally, to the structure of *Inception*. The three concepts are the Pledge, the Turn and the Prestige. The Pledge is that first stage of any trick when a magician presents his equipment or describes the situation and makes it clear to the audience what he will do (what he *pledges* to). This can be made explicit or just hinted at. The Turn is the second stage, during which an action is performed or an event takes place, and something is changed into something else, disappears or behaves in some way unnaturally (e.g. a playing card becomes another playing card, an object vanishes, or a person is sawn in half, etc.). The expression 'Turn' therefore denotes a change of some kind, but it is also of course the common term for an individual theatrical performance. The Prestige is the final stage of the trick, during which something even more remarkable or surprising takes place, often involving a restoration of the original state of affairs, and emphasising the magician's skill and brilliance at creating such illusions (the original playing card is restored, the object reappears, and the person sawn in half is whole again). In the sense in which the term is used in magic it seems to combine both a previously common but now obsolete meaning of the word with the modern usage. Deriving from Latin *praestigium*, it used to mean a 'delusion or illusion', but nowadays, of course, it also carries the connotation of being impressive and having an imposing quality. The film *The Prestige* lives up to its name with a stunning revelation in the final sequence.

The Batman Trilogy

Christian Bale as Batman

Batman Begins (2005)

The audience soon realises that the opening of this film is within a dream. As with the dreams in *Inception*, the start of the dream is not shown: the dreamer is already *in medias res*. The first intimation that it might be a dream comes with the growing sense of the strangeness of the experience. Then there is a sudden cut to Bruce Wayne waking up with a start, and the audience can now guess with some certainty that it was all a dream.

As with Cobb in *Inception*, Wayne (Christian Bale) is plagued by guilt. In this case he feels he is responsible for his parents' deaths. As a child, his fear of the bat-like images of dancing figures in a performance of Arrigo Boito's opera *Mefistofele* causes the family to leave the theatre early. His parents are then set upon by murderous muggers. Wayne has to undergo a process of learning how to control the dark side of his nature, the anger and guilt he feels for his parents' deaths, and incorporate it into a mature ethical self. He is first exposed to the destructive vigilante values of 'The League of Shadows', but eventually learns the importance of justice and compassion. One thing he does retain from his training by 'The League of Shadows' is the realisation that it is sometimes necessary to use tricks and not reveal one's true identity. The character Ducard (Liam Neeson) reminds him, 'Theatricality and deception are powerful agents', and later in the film Wayne accuses Ducard of 'cheap parlour tricks to conceal your true identity'. One is reminded not only of the magic tricks in *The Prestige*, but also of the necessity of deception for the success of the inception process.

There are also clear allusions in the film to specific aspects of Jungian psychology, which are worth analysing. The family butler and factotum, Alfred (Michael Caine), uses the Jungian term 'persona' to describe the Batman role that Wayne adopts 'to protect those you care about'. Jung describes the 'persona' generally in the following terms: 'One could say, with a little exaggeration, that the persona is that which in reality one is not, but which oneself as well as others think one is.'[5] And there is the other figure who dons a mask in the film, Dr. Jonathan Crane (Cillian Murphy). He wears the expressionless, sack-like face of 'The Scarecrow', onto which his victims project their worst fears (Wayne sees bats). Dr. Crane himself draws the connection to Jung: 'Patients suffering delusional episodes often focus their paranoia on an external tormentor, usually one conforming to Jungian archetypes. In this case a scarecrow.' Jung believed that everybody shares what he called 'aboriginal, innate, and inherited shapes of the human mind'. These were 'collective images' and 'mythological motifs'[6] to which he applied the term archetypes. In *Psychological Types* (1921), Jung defines archetypes further as 'the accumulated experiences of organic life in general, a million times repeated, and condensed into types'.[7]

The character of Bruce Wayne in the film also lends itself to analysis in terms of depth psychology. It can be argued that after the loss of his parents, for which he feels responsible, Wayne is constantly seeking new parental role models. Alfred, his butler, incorporates ideal aspects of parenthood in one person: the practical and mindful father, who warns of imminent danger, and the caring, loving mother. Ducard is a stern, misleading father figure for a while, and Lucius (Morgan Freeman) remains throughout a practical father figure on which he can rely. He provides an assurance of security, through his management of the Batman technology. Another important aspect of Wayne's maturation is the overcoming of fear. All his fears are encapsulated in one image, that of bats, and the simple lesson he must learn is that fears can only be overcome by facing them. In his case, rather than repressing them from his consciousness, he identifies with the bats and embodies them in creating the figure of Batman, thus turning his bat complex into a positive force for good. His anxiety is thereby transformed into anger and righteous indignation.

The Dark Knight (2008)

By contrast with *Batman Begins*, the second film in the trilogy does not explore the psychology of the main characters in any complexity. Instead the film deals in polar opposites: good and evil, order and chaos, right and wrong, with the dichotomies being symbolised most visibly perhaps by the 'two-faced' Harvey Dent (Aaron Eckhart), *after* he has been disfigured by fire. From being the city's 'white knight' he has now become a vengeful murderer.

The theme of free will versus chance plays an important role in *The Dark Knight*. Though much in the film can be seen as due to chance events, it is also clear that the strong-willed win through. In relation to this point the recurrent image of 'spinning a coin' is especially important. 'Spinning a coin' is traditionally a way of allowing chance to determine human action. It is thus a way of avoiding the responsibility of choice. On one occasion of 'coin-tossing' in the film, Rachel (Maggie Gyllenhaal) asserts 'You make your own luck', which of course implies the role of will in taking advantage of circumstances. For the Joker (Heath Ledger), who is described in the film as 'the agent of chaos', there is no role for moral choice. Later in the film he says: 'The only morality in a cruel world is chance.' Thus, for the Joker, individual will and chance predominate over any sense of right and wrong.

Inception, on the other hand, presents a more mechanistic view of the mind: situations are constructed and manipulated, and the will can be undermined by implanting alternative ideas and desires. Free will is seen to be essentially an illusion, and conscious decisions and actions can be determined by subconscious thoughts.

In relation to one of the design aspects of *The Dark Knight*, there is evidence of Nolan's interest in the work of the British artist, Francis Bacon. It will be remembered that homage is paid to Bacon in *Inception*, by the inclusion of one of his works in a room of the Japanese castle (see chapter 7). Nolan has said of the make-up for the Joker: 'We gave a Francis Bacon spin to [his face]. This corruption, this decay in the texture of the look itself. It's grubby. You can almost imagine what he smells like.'[8] There is another point of comparison with the work of Bacon in the film. When the 'white knight' Harvey Dent is severely burnt and becomes 'Two-face', the left side of his face is horribly disfigured – large areas, especially that around the mouth, reveal the bone and sinew structure beneath.

The Dark Knight Rises (2012)

The third film in the trilogy closely follows and continues developments in the preceding two films, with many of the same actors. Two notable new characters who are important in initiating plot developments are the cat burglar Selina Kyle (Anne Hathaway) and the destructively brutal figure of Bane (Tom Hardy), who is a mercenary obsessed with destroying Gotham City. Various modifications were made to features established in the previous two films. Most notably the 'Batplane' was developed, and a new 'Batcave' set was created.

Despite the fact that Harvey Dent committed crimes in *The Dark Knight*, the so-called 'Dent Act' has been effective in nearly eradicating organised crime in the city. Police Commissioner Gordon (Gary Oldman) decides not to reveal the truth about Dent. And Bruce Wayne has become a recluse, while his 'alter ego', Batman, has disappeared. It is the action of Bane in attacking the Gotham City Stock Exchange which provokes

Wayne into resurrecting his Batman identity. The rest of the plot is intricate and it is only necessary to relate the salient developments here, which bear on ideological and moral aspects of the events in the film.

A central part of the plot concerns a project undertaken by Wayne Enterprises: the building of a fusion reactor. One assumes that this was to have peaceful aims, because Wayne is prepared to let the company become unprofitable when he cancels the project on learning that the core could be utilised as a nuclear weapon. The reactor is to feature prominently at the climax of the film when Bane abducts a physicist, Dr. Leonid Pavel, and forces him to convert it into a nuclear bomb. Bane's subsequent actions reveal his aim of setting up autocratic, dictatorial control of Gotham City under the guise of an anti-capitalist revolution. He holds the whole city to ransom with his bomb, embodying thus in blatant form the methodology of extreme fascism: follow his dictates or suffer the consequences. He debases the idealised figure of Harvey Dent by revealing his crimes and undoes the effects of the 'Dent Act' by releasing all the prisoners from the main penitentiary. This effectively initiates a revolution and renders the justice system powerless. The rich and powerful people of the city have their property seized and they are submitted to show trials, presided over by Dr. Jonathan Crane. The death sentence is a foregone conclusion.

Wayne Enterprises board member Miranda Tate (Marion Cotillard) has been revealed to be the daughter, Talia, of the leader of The League of Shadows, Ra's al Ghul, who is the real author of the plan to destroy Gotham City. Before she dies, when her truck crashes, Tate/Talia destroys the reactor, making it impossible to prevent the detonation of the bomb. Batman now becomes the selfless saviour: he apparently sacrifices himself for the sake of the city by flying the bomb out to sea, where it explodes. We learn from Alfred, however, that he has survived.

The importance of considering the sequence of the main events in the film is that they demonstrate its central moral stance: as long as unprincipled evil is manifest in some form in the city, then concerned vigilantes, who act outside the law, such as Batman, will be necessary to protect society. There is a strong hint at the end of the film that, whatever the fate of this particular vigilante, Batman, there will continue to be a need for some such defender of the innocent. And the young officer, Blake

(Joseph Gordon-Levitt), who has resigned from the police force, seems set to inherit the role, through his discovery of the Batcave. It is no coincidence that his first name is revealed to be Robin...

The apparent approval of vigilantism in the film has led some critics to suggest that it has a politically conservative agenda. Catherine Shoard, of *The Guardian*, describes the film as having 'a quite audaciously capitalist vision, radically conservative, radically vigilante'.[9] But Nolan insists that the film was not intended to be overtly political: 'What we're really trying to do is show the cracks of society, show the conflicts that somebody would try to wedge open.'[10]

There is also some suggestion of support for traditional family values in the film. Alfred, Wayne's faithful butler and father figure, talks to him of his dream for Bruce to eventually lead a normal life of marital fulfillment within a family. At the end of the film this appears to be realised, or about to be realised, when Arthur sees him with a woman across a street café, just as he had envisioned it earlier. It is a similar 'dream' of normal family life which drives Cobb in *Inception*. After his wife's death he is dominated by the desire to get back to the remains of his family life, his children and his wife's parents, in the USA.

In the early part of *The Dark Knight Rises*, a safe, in Wayne's mansion, plays a significant symbolic role. The jewel thief (Selina Kyle) steals Bruce's identity (his fingerprints) from the safe. It can be interpreted as a violation of his private identity. In *Inception*, of course, a safe and a vault play even more significant roles as depositories for secret information about the individuals to whom they belong: in the Japanese castle belonging to Saito, in Mal's room and in the hospital room of the mountain fortress, where Fischer's father lies dying.

If the audience has the patience to wade through all the credits at the end of the film, they will also discover a statement which expresses an essential part of Nolan's philosophy of film production: 'This motion picture was shot and finished on film.' In other words, it was not made with the use of digital media.

Interstellar (2014)

Matthew McConaughey, *Interstellar*

This film was made subsequent to *Inception* and it pursues some of the ideas and themes touched upon in that film in different directions. There is a more detailed exploration, for example, of moral values, including concerns about conflicts between individual needs and those of humanity as a whole. One should be wary of viewing the film entirely as an 'auteur' production, however, as, due to the exigencies of the Hollywood studio system, Nolan was not involved in the project from the outset. The original scenario was conceived by film producer Lynda Obst and theoretical physicist Kip Thorne. Then Steven Spielberg became interested in directing, but was eventually unavailable. Paramount hired Nolan. The first part of the script is very much a re-write by his brother Jonathan, but Christopher developed his own ideas in the second part of the film.[11]

A central theme in *Interstellar* is the necessity of deception of those one loves for the sake of knowledge and of the concerns of humanity as a whole. There is an obvious point of comparison with Cobb's experimenting on his wife in *Inception*, which leaves him riddled with guilt when she commits suicide. In *Interstellar* Professor Brand (Michael Caine) deceives both the astronaut Cooper (Matthew McConaughey) and his own daughter (Anne Hathaway), leading them to believe that by undertaking an expedition through a wormhole they will be able to save those people they love. In fact Brand's aim is to realise 'plan B': to breed a new race of humans for fertilizing embryos on a new planet. Deception is also central to the twists in *The Prestige*, in which science is seen as the 'real magic'. The idea of technology as magic is clearly in Cooper's mind in *Interstellar*, when, after accomplishing a particularly difficult manoeuvre in his spaceship, he exclaims: 'And now for my next trick!'

Scientific theories of time are also explored more thoroughly in *Interstellar* than in *Inception*. In *Inception* the participants experience time as passing at different speeds according to which level of dreaming they are on. In *Interstellar* the astronauts age more slowly in interstellar space than their families on Earth. A planet on which the crew lands is near a black hole, and one of them ages significantly during the time it takes the others to explore. Near the end of the film Professor Brand says that he is more afraid of time than he is of death.

A unique theme in *Interstellar*, not treated by Nolan in his other films to date, occurs in the latter part of the film: a mystical identification of gravity and love is developed. And there is also included the notion of beings which exist in more than three dimensions. Common to both *Interstellar* and *Inception*, especially in their conclusions, is the view that one must overcome a love which is tied to an irretrievable past and try to find love with the living.

Dunkirk (2017)

The latest film by Nolan, at the time of writing, was *Dunkirk*. He wrote, co-produced and directed the film, a UK-USA-France-Netherlands co-production. The plot, such as it is, is clear and simple. It focuses entirely on the evacuation from Dunkirk of Allied troops in 1940. After the Allies attempted to invade France they were driven back to the small seaside town of Dunkirk. As the German forces closed in, the Allied troops waited desperately to be evacuated.

Kenneth Branagh, *Dunkirk*

There are clear parallels which can be drawn between *Dunkirk* and *Inception* with regard to the experience of passing time. In *Inception*, there are three levels of time within the dreams, with a fourth deeper level referred to as limbo, which involves the eventual breakdown of all consciousness into a state of chaos. In the first level of a dream, time is experienced as being longer than that in normal waking life, although it takes up the same amount of normal waking time. In the first dream within a dream, time is experienced as being even longer still, and in the third level (the dream within a dream within a dream), the length of experienced time is even greater still. There are parts of Inception in which there are cuts to and fro between the various dream states, giving the impressions that the events are all taking place simultaneously.

In *Dunkirk* also three levels of action take place concurrently but over different lengths of time. The action on land covers a period of one week. In the film it bears the title 'The Mole'. The sequence entitled 'The Sea' focuses on the endeavours of a Mr. Dawson (Mark Rylance), together with his son Peter and hand George, to reach Dunkirk in their small boat. It covers a period of one day. Finally the section entitled 'The Air' relates the attempts of three pilots to cross the Channel in their Spitfires. The action covers a period of one hour. All three sequences are intercut, enabling the creation of frequent moments of suspense. Of course, in reality they would overlap in time, but due to the intercutting the three sequences are experienced as occurring concurrently. The effect of this is, of course, is to emphasise how the characters in each sequence actually experience the time: the long waiting on the beach for the evacuation, the hard struggle to get across the Channel in a small boat, and the speed with which the aerial dogfights are enacted.

A typical Nolan feature in the film is the use of a final ambiguous image (cf. the endings of *The Prestige* and *Inception* especially). In *Dunkirk* the young man Tommy (Fionn Whitehead) has been reading aloud to his companion from a newspaper the words of Churchill's 'we shall fight on the beaches' speech. This technique thus conveys in a subtle way the sense of the British war-time prime minister's words without letting his oratorical style disrupt the tenor of the film. Tommy looks up from the paper and we see his face briefly. That is all. There is no clear indication of what he is feeling after reading the newspaper report. Nolan imposes the onus of interpretation entirely on the audience. Is he pleased, is he confused, is he in disbelief? Is he thinking how far removed Churchill's noble words are from the realities of the actual experience of the event? Tommy's gaze reveals nothing of his own thoughts, but challenges ours.

3. The Industrial Context of *Inception*: From Production to Premiere

Nolan first tried out his treatment for *Inception* with Warner Bros. after making *Memento*, but then realised the scope that would be required for the film and decided to gain more experience making large-scale films.[12] After completing *The Dark Knight* Nolan finally decided to make *Inception* and spent the next six months completing the script. The first actor to be cast in the film as the protagonist, Cobb, Leonardo DiCaprio.[13] Nolan had known DiCaprio for some years and had approached him unsuccessfully several times. DiCaprio finally agreed to do *Inception* because he was 'intrigued by the concept'.[14] In the 'Production Notes' issued by Warner Bros. DiCaprio is quoted as saying that it was the driving force embodied in the central character that drew him to the script: 'It is this highly entertaining, complex thriller where anything can happen, but at the heart is one man's quest to uncover a long-buried truth and to get back home.'[15] Nolan spent many months discussing the screenplay with DiCaprio and took a long time re-writing the script, 'to make sure that the emotional journey of his character was the driving force of the movie'.[16] Emma Thomas, Nolan's wife and producer, stresses that they knew from the start that the production was going to be a big one. The scope of it would be bigger than anything they had undertaken before, 'just in terms of the number of countries in which we shot'.[17] In fact the filming took place in six different countries and on four separate continents. The main locations were in the UK, Morocco, Canada, Tokyo, Paris and Los Angeles. Nolan has stressed that they deliberately filmed in six different countries, building enormous sets because he was interested in 'pushing the boundaries of what could be achieved practically, as opposed to computer effects'.[18]

The other main actors have also expressed their reasons for wanting to work on the film. Ellen Page has said: 'It was so conceptually original and so incredibly moving, with a powerful emotional spine that one can really connect to it.'[19] Ken Watanabe said he had welcomed the opportunity to work with a director he had enjoyed working with before.[20] Cillian Murphy was mainly pleased to be working with the other well-known actors.[21] Marion Cotillard talked of her need for a director she could trust, 'someone to take your hand and share his vision'.[22]

Nolan was concerned to gather several of his previous collaborators together to make up his crew for the film. These included Wally Pfister, as director of photography, Lee Smith as editor, Chris Corbould for special effects, and Paul Franklin as his visual effects supervisor. His stunt coordinator was Tom Struthers. He required all of his crew to achieve as many of their effects as possible in practical terms, by which he meant keeping computer graphic effects to the minimum. This is important because he felt it was crucial when creating dream worlds 'that, at every level, the world feels concrete because when we are in a dream, we accept it as reality'.[23] The result was that a large amount of the cinematography was completed on location.

Concerns for realism also governed Nolan's choice of cameras and film. The film was shot primarily in the anamorphic format on 35 mm film, with some key sequences filmed on 65 mm. He did not shoot any footage with IMAX cameras because he felt that it did not suit his ideal of realism.[24] Sequences in slow motion were filmed on a Photo-Sonics 35 mm camera at speeds of up to 1,000 frames per second. He did not want to shoot the film in 3D as he prefers shooting on film using prime lenses, which is not possible with 3D cameras.[25]

Warner Bros. spent $100 million marketing the film because it trusted Nolan as a brand.[26] They also endeavoured to maintain an air of secrecy about the film, but released teasing trailers featuring an animated spinning top. They also set up an online game called 'Mind Crime', and devised various other gimmicks and online attractions.[27]

Inception was released on July 10, 2010, and its opening weekend gross takings made it the second-highest grossing debut for a science fiction film that was not a sequel or remake (the highest being *Avatar* in 2009).

4. The Question of Genre

Nolan changed his mind several times about what kind of film he wanted to make. This led him to view the material at different times in terms of different genres. He has said that he initially imagined developing the general idea as a horror film, and wrote an 80-page treatment about dream-stealers.[28] As he set about writing it he came to view it more as a heist film, though even at this early stage he had reservations about conceiving it in this genre: 'traditionally [heist films] are very deliberately superficial in emotional terms.'[29] It is thus clear that he was starting to envision something with psychological depth. Basing it in the heist genre would not work because his story 'relies so heavily on the idea of the interior state, the idea of dream and memory. I realised I needed to raise the emotional stakes.'[30] This involved no quick fix and it took him nine to ten years to work on the script.[31] He realised that the development of the central character Cobb was crucial: he wanted 'to make sure that the emotional journey of his character was the driving force of the movie'.[32] This 'emotional journey' of Cobb will be analysed in a subsequent section.

While he was working on the script, Nolan also became aware of contemporary films which had fantasy and science-fiction elements: '...that era of movies where you had *The Matrix* (1999), you had *Dark City* (1998), you had *The Thirteenth Floor* (1999)... They were based in the principles that the world around you might not be real.'[33] *Inception* was to share one quality with pure fantasy films: anything you can imagine should be possible. In Nolan's words: '...as soon as you're talking about dreams, the potential of the human mind is infinite. And so the scale of the film has to feel infinite. It has to feel like you could go anywhere by the end of film. And it has to work on a massive scale.'[34] An important link with many sci-fi films was also maintained: the notion of alternative universes. This came about when Nolan started to consider what effects would ensue if several people could share the same dream: 'Once you remove the privacy, you've created an infinite number of alternative universes in which people can meaningfully interact, with validity, with weight, with dramatic consequences.'[35] His choice of words here is significant: 'validity', 'weight', and 'dramatic consequences'. These qualities presuppose one particular feature of the dream world, which is emphasised several times in the film, specifically by Cobb: the dream seems real as long as you are in it, and you interact meaningfully with other persons in the dream.

It is debatable whether the term 'film noir' can be perceived as referring to a genre or to characteristics of films in various genres. Paul Meehan has drawn attention to the lack of agreement among critics on this point: 'Some critics maintain that noir is only a matter of style, a set of visual conventions that define the genre such as high-contrast lighting, unusual camera angles, etc.'[36] In the same study he has made the point more generally: 'It has been said that noir is not a genre, but a way of looking at the world.'[37] It is certainly possible to perceive some 'film noir' elements in *Inception*. Daryl Lee, in his study *The Heist Film, Stealing with Style* (2014), has pointed out that many examples of heist films, especially the early ones, can also be described as noir films.[38] Most notably, *Inception* features prominently the noir topos of the 'femme fatale'. Cobb's wife Mal (Marion Cotillard) appears as a projection by him which he cannot control and which constantly threatens to thwart all his endeavours. Nolan himself has described her as 'the essence of the femme fatale'.[39]

To avoid applying terms such as 'heist' and 'sci-fi' in too facile a way to the film, it will be useful to reflect on the notion of genre in general, how best to identify and describe genres, and then on the characteristics of the heist and sci-fi genres in particular.

The Notion of Genre

Early in his book, *Film/Genre* (1999), Rick Altman quotes from another theorist, Richard T. Jameson, who edited a collection of essays which attempted to redefine film genres. Jameson's perceptions are worth re-quoting:

> Movies belong to genres much the way people belong to families or ethnic groups. Name one of the classic, bedrock genres – Western, comedy, musical, war film, gangster picture, science fiction, horror – and even the most casual moviegoer will come up with a mental image of it, partly visual, partly conceptual.[40]

The terms 'partly visual, partly conceptual' do indeed characterise well how our minds focus when attempting to allocate genre to a specific film.

If we are to judge whether *Inception* belongs to a specific genre or shares qualities with several genres, then it is necessary to have a clearer and more precise notion of what a genre is, a workable methodology which can be applied in order to characterise a film. Often discussed and probably still the best workable methodology currently available is the 'semantic/syntactic approach' defined by Rick Altman, first in an article in *Cinema Journal 23*,[41] and then developed more fully by him in *Film/Genre*. This approach will be explained shortly. Altman has a style which is often difficult to penetrate, involving much quasi-philosophical and linguistic quibbling, but his arguments produce eventually some sound and useful principles.

Before explaining the approach, it is important to bear in mind Altman's own reservations. In the concluding chapter to his book Altman recognises the shortcomings of his original approach but still finds it useful:

> ...the semantic/syntactic approach may serve analytic purposes admirably, offering a satisfying descriptive vocabulary useful for interpreting individual texts and relating them to existing generic groupings.[42]

One factor that he felt he had overlooked was the importance of audience perspective: 'I underemphasised the fact that genres look different to different audiences.'[43]

He is finally forced to conclude that genre, like many words in all languages, cannot be defined precisely:

> Instead of a word or a category capable of clear and stable definition (the goal of previous genre theorists), genre has been presented as a multivalent term multiply and variously valorized by various user groups.[44]

Despite these reservations in the later book, Altman's concepts outlined in the earlier article remain a useful tool, if rough and ready, to help provide a descriptive framework for any film considered for inclusion in a given genre.

The semantic/syntactic approach

The abstract concept 'semantic/syntactic approach' refers in fact to a straightforward practical approach, which is easy to grasp. A semantic definition depends 'on a list of common traits, attitudes, characters, shots, locations, set and the like'.[45] A syntactic definition emphasises 'certain constitutive relationships between undesignated and variable place-holders – relationships that might be called the genre's fundamental syntax'.[46] Semantic thus refers to the elements of meaning in a film, and syntactic refers to the structural principles employed in joining these elements together into a meaningful whole. In Altman's words: 'the semantic approach thus stresses the genre's building blocks, while the syntactic view privileges the structures into which they are arranged.'[47] Many theorists had previously taken one or the other approach to establish the generic identity of a film. Altman argues 'that these two categories of generic analysis are complementary, that they can be combined'.[48] Not only *can* they be combined, but to account fully for the nature of any film, they *must* be combined:

It is simply not possible to describe Hollywood cinema accurately without the ability to account for the numerous films that innovate by combining the syntax of one genre with the semantics of another.[49]

Change and development of a genre is envisioned as occurring in the following way:

...either a relatively stable set of semantic givens is developed through syntactic experimentation into a coherent and durable syntax, or an already existing syntax adopts a new set of semantic elements.[50]

He cites as an example the recent history of the Hollywood sci-fi film:

At first defined only by a relatively stable science fiction semantics, the genre first begins borrowing the syntactic relationships previously established by the horror film, only to move in recent years increasingly towards the syntax of the Western.[51]

It is interesting to note that in his 1984 article Altman did not consider what he called the 'big caper films' (i.e. grand scale heist films) as constituting a successful distinctive genre. He classed them among 'those that disappear the quickest' because they 'depend entirely on recurring semantic elements, never developing a stable syntax'.[52]

The Heist Film Genre

Many films have focused on crimes of various kinds as their main subject matter. What has become known as a heist film is a particular kind of crime film, in which the main interest of the storyline is the planning, execution and aftermath of a theft of some kind. If there are a considerable number of comic elements in the film it is often referred to as a 'caper' film. There may be many twists in the plots, and suspense is often created by unexpected delays, hindrances and other threats to the accomplishment of the main task. The theft must often be carried out in opposition to a figure of authority or organisation, such as the police force or large company, etc. The ending of a heist film usually involves a morally satisfying outcome: if the theft is carried out for purely selfish motives against a respectable authority, then more often than not the thieves will be caught and suffer punishment of some kind. But if the authority is corrupt or indeed itself criminal, then the thieves often gain our sympathy and indeed escape punishment.

For a concise analysis of the development of the heist film the reader is referred to *The Heist Film*, *Stealing with Style*, (2014), by Daryl Lee, which examines why directors of all kinds, from studio based to independents, have been attracted to the genre. Lee traces its development from early noir films such as *Criss Cross* (1949), *The Killers* (1946) and *The Asphalt Jungle* (1950), through so-called 'capers' such as the original *Ocean's Eleven* (1960), *How to Steal a Million* (1966) and *Gambit* (1966), culminating in the recent spate of remakes, such as that of *Ocean's Eleven* (2001) and *The Italian Job* (2003, the remake inspired by the original 1969 film). In his final chapter Lee also considers the status of *Inception* as a heist film. His conclusion is that in the last few decades the heist film has been used especially to express a critique of mainstream social values:

> By far the majority of heist films since the 1990s enjoy some successful outcome against society, oppressive institutions or mainstream morality. In other words, the cultural mood across the period may have invited filmmakers to reshape a genre that, at its origin, had typically ended in failure.[53]

The most prominent semantic features of a heist film, apart from the nature of the object to be stolen and the nature of the authority or organisation against which the heist is committed, are the characters of the perpetrators, the gang or team. Stuart Kaminsky has argued that there are two main types, together with various other individuals. First there is the gang leader, a man of action (rarely a woman), and then there is the mentor or mastermind who plans the whole enterprise. Occasionally these are blended into one character. The other team members have 'individual skills and crafts which command no great social respect and which have little or no chance of making those who possess them wealthy by any legal metho'd'[54]

Syntactically, the heist film usually has a basic three-act storyline: the planning and preparation of the heist, followed by its actual execution, and culminating in either the failure or success of the heist and retribution if apposite.

Inception as Heist Film

A noticeable feature of *Inception* is that it contains two heists, a short minor one and the main heist which takes up the major part of the film. They are demonstrably related. The first is in fact a more genuine heist, in that it involves an attempted robbery of something, whereas the second and main heist, while having many characteristics of the heist, in fact involves the planting rather than the removal of something. It can be argued that if anything is stolen it is a man's freedom of choice.

The first heist involves the attempt to steal information from a safe in a castle in Japan belonging to the industrialist Saito. We are not shown the whole process as in a conventional heist film, but are suddenly immersed in the action n media res during the carrying out of the heist. Little is explained about the background and motives and we must pick up the gist of the situation from hints in the dialogue and action. Suspense is created, as usual in this genre, by unexpected delays and hindrances, most notably those caused by the mysterious figure of Mal intervening at various stages to thwart Cobb's intentions. In one sequence he has to resort to tying her to a chair in order to escape from her through a window, only to discover that she has somehow slipped her bonds. The central figure, perpetrator and organiser appears to be Cobb, who is working with the aid of a few other men who are only sketchily identified at this stage of the film. There is no evidence of any separate mentor or mastermind behind the process.

The outcome of this first heist is unconventional in that, while as an operation it may have failed, it is revealed to be what Saito describes as an 'audition'. It has not been a heist in the 'real world', but a process induced in the mind of Saito in order to access information he is keeping secret. This process is known as extraction. The 'audition' itself is successful, because it has revealed to Saito that Cobb is capable of creating and acting in dreams within dreams. This capability is necessary for the process of inception, the implanting of a motivating idea in the subconscious mind. He is now ready to make an offer to Cobb: enabling him to return to his family in return for the performance of inception, the second 'heist'.

The second and extensive heist forms the main part of the film, and it follows the traditional heist format more closely. There is first the bringing together of a skilled gang. There is Arthur (Joseph Gordon-Levitt), who is already a trusted side-kick, and then Eames (Tom Hardy) is introduced, who provides some dubious but necessary skills, including those of forgery and impersonation. There is also Yusuf (Dileep Rao), who is an expert chemist and provides the specific pharmaceutical compound which is able to induce the necessary dream state. He is also the driver of the white van in the first level of the dream, and thus comparable to the 'getaway driver' in classic heists. Then there is the brilliant young student Ariadne (Ellen Page), whom Cobb needs to design the architecture of the dreams for him, because if he does it himself, his subconscious projection of his wife Mal will also have knowledge of it and be able to pursue him. It is rare in heist films that women play central roles in carrying out the theft. Ariadne insists in taking part to ensure the success of the enterprise, as only she is familiar with the complexity of the architecture and also to some extent with Cobb's psychological complexity. Apart from her, only Arthur knows about Cobb's problematic relationship with his wife. There is a mentor of sorts in the film, though he condones Cobbs actions only reluctantly, and is thus not part of the team. This is Miles (Michael Caine), Cobb's father-in-law and Ariadne's professor. He also taught Cobb the techniques involved in the construction of dream architecture.

The figure of authority against whom the team is working is Fischer senior, head of a global business enterprise, which if allowed to gain a dominant position, will have dire consequences for the world. It is the mind of his son, Robert (Cillian Murphy), who is due to inherit the enterprise, which they must change. And suspense is maintained in the film through the constant threats from the manifestations of Mal, bent on disrupting Cobb's plans, and from the so-called sub-security, the defence mechanisms in Robert's subconscious, which fight to protect his mind from invasion by the team.

In keeping with more recent examples of heist films, the audience has sympathy with the perpetrators. After successfully performing inception, the team escapes alive, Saito is rescued from limbo and then enables Cobb to return to his family. It is thus also a conventional happy ending, or is at least ambiguously so.

Lee suggests that Nolan's film can be perceived as an allegory of film-making itself. While the comparison is not explicit in the film it can be made with regard to certain aspects: 'Inception casts the filmmaker as a master thief and formulates the "shared dreaming" of its thieves as an allegory of cinematic creation and reception.'[55] The rest of Lee's commentary on the film needs to be read critically, and with close comparison to the film. He makes some perceptive observations on the timeless nature of the spaces in which the action occurs: 'the very spaces in which the film's travelers carry out their central heist; spaces in which neither identity, nor relations, nor history really makes any sense.'[56] But then in speculating about the time frames of the film, he wrongly identifies two levels rather than three levels of dreaming. And he also describes Cobb's and Mal's 'imaginary dream city' as 'thoroughly contemporary', failing to note the inclusion of old buildings with personal associations. This enables him to conclude that 'Inception revives the zeitgeist and urban spirit of the original noir heist'.[57]

The Sci-fi Film Genre

It is important to note that, as with all film genres, sci-fi cannot be described as though it were a static phenomenon. There is no scope here for a detailed history of the genre, but various published studies have indicated clearly the main lines of its development. For example, the aptly titled The Rough Guide to Sci-fi Movies (2005) by John Scalzi, does indeed provide a rough outline of the development of the genre, but it is a sound one. In the second chapter, after a survey of the 'The Silent Era' (1902-29), the account continues with emphases on the main themes and recurring tropes of different periods. Thus for the 1930s and 40s it notes the preoccupation with mad scientists and the prevalence of serials. The 1950s were 'the Golden Age of sci-fi film', reflecting international concerns about atomic weapons and the Cold War. Between 1960 and 1976 'Sci-fi film grows up', with the first few years of the 1960s very much continuing the themes of the 1950s. But by the mid-60s 'edgy and avant-garde directors had begun to play with the genre'.[58] As the 1970s progressed 'the recurrent themes in science fiction were dark ones: technology running amuck, and the future of humanity spinning out of control'.[59] Scalzi notes that 1977 was the year of the first *Star Wars*, initiating what he describes as 'the new era of spectacle'.[60] The 1990s marks for him the beginning of the 'Digital Era'.[61] For the beginning of the 21st century he registers no dominant themes but emphasises the importance of 'cutting edge effects' and the fact that sci-films were being aimed more at an international market.[62]

Despite the multiplicity of themes and changes in the modes of treating them over time, it *is* possible to list some of the most popular and long-established semantic elements of sci-fi films. This list, in no special order, is by no means exhaustive: alien worlds and life-forms, space travel, robots and cyborgs, time travel, modifications of the human body and mind, future worlds, interfaces between humans and computers, parallel worlds, superheroes, boundaries between science, magic and the supernatural, natural and man-made disasters, monster life forms, explanations by the use of imaginary/speculative science, teleportation, invisibility, etc. It is also possible to classify certain recurrent character types as semantic elements: the mad, or at least obsessive scientist; the righteous hero who saves humanity, or at least his part of it; the beautiful but vulnerable woman; the practical, supportive (through physical or mental ability) male companion; the computer geek; the arch-villain; the selfish and powerful person concerned only to maintain his/her standing, to name but a few.

Concerning the syntactic structure of sci-fi films there is again considerable variety, but many reveal variations on certain basic situations and storylines. To name a few: a team of people struggling to combat alien life forms with the final triumph of human values; a similar situation but with robots or cyborgs instead of alien life forms; struggle for survival in an imaginary or alien world, with a man and a woman, who, after trials and tribulations, learn to respect each other, and frequently fall in love, etc.

Inception as Sci-fi Film

Concerning the film's semantic elements, it certainly incorporates much speculative science, concerning the nature of consciousness, dreams, and the human mind in general. It also has as a central focus the nature of the experience of time at different levels on the conscious and unconscious mind. And it features speculative technology: the mysterious machine which somehow enables several people to share the same dream states by the application of a mind-altering drug (never adequately explained). Fundamental to the whole process of inception is the assumption that the human mind can be controlled and its motivations modified. The film also features a fantastic journey through an imaginary world, in this case one consisting of artificially generated dreams, with designer landscapes and persons (the transformations of Eames). The leader of the team which sets out to perform inception is also persuaded to perceive their task as saving the world, albeit not from an alien force but from the selfish concerns of a big conglomerate.

Common sci-fi syntactic elements in the film are a long exposition sequence including the training of a specialist team, the fantastic journey with its trials and tribulations (the destructive threats of the various manifestations of sub-security and of Cobb's projection of his wife Mal), the development of the relationship between the central man with a mission and the woman who supports him (Ariadne), a race against time to achieve a goal which will save humanity, and the re-establishment of a state of normality at the end.

Other Sci-fi Films with Points of Comparison

There have been many films in the history of cinema which have featured exploration of the human mind and have attempted to evoke the experience of dreams. There have also been some which have involved entering into and controlling the process of dreaming. In this context I am considering only a selection of films which are worth comparing with *Inception*, either to reveal similarities or to contrast their concepts of mind and dreaming.

In the early British film *The Man Who Changed His Mind* (1936), directed by Robert Stevenson, a scientist, played by the inimitable Boris Karloff, conducts research into the nature of the mind and the reality of the soul. He starts to experiment with brain transference, and first exchanges the mind of a rich philanthropist with that of a cripple, gaining mastery over the philanthropist's wealth. Then he exchanges his own mind with that of the philanthopist's handsome son in order to seduce his own assistant, Clare. There are obvious similarities to the various versions of the *Frankenstein* story, but the focus is on the attempts to control another's man's mind. In this case dreams do not play a role in the process.

Extensive developments in the technology of cinematography have meant that it has become possible in recent decades to create more easily convincing dreamlike sequences in films. An example of this is the film *Dreamscape* (1984; not to be confused with another film with the same title, but not a remake, of 2007, and which will be considered shortly). A scientist, Novotny, involved in government-funded research, has developed a technique which enables psychic persons to project themselves into the subconscious minds of others while they are asleep. Although the technique employed is different, there are obvious points of comparison with the procedure adopted in *Inception*. The scientist's original aim in *Dreamscape* was a benevolent one, to diagnose and treat sleep disorders, especially nightmares, but the project is hijacked by a government agent, named Blair, who plans to use the technique to perform an assassination. The storyline also includes a sequence in which the young psychic, Alex, played by Dennis Quaid, sneaks into the dream of Novotny's fellow scientist, Clare, and has sex with her. When the US President is admitted to the clinic to have treatment for his own nightmares, Blair arranges for a psychopath to be sent into the president's nightmare in an attempt to assassinate him, but Alex manages to project himself into the President's dream and saves him. Finally Alex also enters Blair's dream to prevent him from pursuing his murderous plans further. The film also utilises the shape-changing facility found in many dreams, and which Eames takes advantage of in *Inception*. In *Dreamscape* the psychopath adopts the appearance of a snake-like monster from another patient's nightmares, and Alex takes on the appearance of the psychopath's own father. Another point of comparison between the two films occurs in the final sequence of *Dreamscape*. As in *Inception* the audience is left uncertain about whether the central characters are in normal reality or in a dream world: the conductor whom Alex and Jane encounter on a train is played by the same actor as the one in Jane's dream.

In an episode of the TV series *The Twilight Zone*, first broadcast in 1985, and entitled 'Dreams For Sale', a woman discovers that what she thought was reality is in fact an induced dream state. She is having an outdoor picnic with her family when she notices that there is a strange stuttering effect in some sounds and things she sees, and some events repeat themselves. She wakes up to find out that she is in a dream-making machine, along with hundreds of others in similar machines in a sterile, otherwise lifeless world. A technician fixes the technical hitch in her machine and she returns to the dream world, which she accepts as her preferred reality. But the machine breaks down and she is trapped permanently in the alternative world. One might make comparisons here with the danger of permanent entrapment in the state of limbo which threatens the team in *Inception*.

Dreams (1990), by Japanese director Akira Kurosawa, consists of eight stories based on dreams which the director himself experienced at different stages in his life. While much of the atmosphere and especially the use of colour in the film may be described as dreamlike, it shares little else with the theme or content of *Inception*. Nevertheless it is interesting to compare the way it depicts the experience of being in a dream with that in Nolan's film, if only to contrast two completely different cinematographic approaches. In the same year an American film appeared which has much more in common with *Inception*. Directed by Paul Verhoeven, and starring Arnold Schwarzenegger, *Total Recall* tells the story of a construction worker, Douglas Quaid, who has disturbing dreams about being on Mars and a mysterious woman he encounters there. In an effort to investigate the source of these dreams he turns to a company called 'Rekall', which provides memory implants of fantasy vacations. He selects a memory trip to Mars as a secret agent. During the procedure something goes wrong, and it becomes unclear whether what Quaid is experiencing is an induced memory, that is to say whether he is hallucinating, or whether it is a real memory of actual events. Previously suppressed memories of actually being a secret agent occur. The company sedates him and wipes his memory before sending him home. But it is soon revealed that his marriage has also been a false memory implant. It is not necessary to relate the subsequent complexities of the plot here, but there are interesting points of comparison with *Inception* in the film's transitions between 'normal reality' and the world of dreams and in the confusion between memories of actual events and artificially induced memories. In both films dreams are used to influence a man's thought and actions. Just as the spinning top in the last shot of *Inception* leaves the audience wondering whether what they are seeing is reality or a dream, so the ending of *Total Recall* teases the audience with its suggestion that Quaid might still be dreaming.

Dark City (1998) evokes a nightmarish world which is a completely artificial reality. No recognisably ordinary reality is presented with which it can be contrasted. Much of what happens involves changing both identities and the physical appearance of the world itself, so that it has much in common with the world of dreams. There are some mysterious figures, referred to as the Strangers, who can stop time and physically rearrange the city as well as change people's memories and their very identities. At one point in the film it is explained that the Strangers are extraterrestrial parasites which share a collective memory. Their survival as a species is threatened and they are studying humanity in the hope that it will provide a means for them to perpetuate themselves. The film does end on an optimistic note with the creation of an alternative world outside the city where the sun shines, but this can still be interpreted as another kind of dream world. Obvious points of comparison with *Inception* can be found in the process of altering people's minds and the manipulation of urban landscapes.

The last film made by Stanley Kubrick, *Eyes Wide Shut* (1999), and based on the Viennese author Arthur Schnitzler's novella *Dream Story* of 1926, is dreamlike throughout, as is the source material. Kubrick transferred the story from Vienna to New York. After learning that his wife had been contemplating having an affair, Dr. Bill Harford becomes involved in various mysterious adventures, including a masked orgy organised by an unnamed secret society. Imperceptibly the film has moved steadily from a world in which normal social behaviour prevails into one of fantasy. After the extravagances of the night Harford returns to his wife and they are able to re-establish their relationship with greater understanding of their mutual needs. The mask which Harford wore at the orgy appears at the end of the film on the pillow next to his sleeping wife, leaving the audience to wonder, as in *Inception*, what has been real and what part of an extensive dream.

Also released in 1999 was *The Thirteenth Floor*, directed by Josef Rusnak. Set in contemporary Los Angeles, it tells of a wealthy inventor and owner of a computer enterprise, Hannon Fuller, who has developed a virtual reality simulation of 1937 Los Angeles, which has been filled with simulated human beings who are unaware that they are in fact computer programs. Fuller is murdered, and his protégé and heir, Douglas Hall becomes the prime suspect. As the film progresses Hall becomes more and more disorientated on discovering that his world consists of virtual reality within virtual reality, rather like dreams within dreams. He discovers first that the Los Angeles of 1990 is itself also a simulation. Jane, the estranged daughter of Fuller, explains to him that his world is one of thousands of virtual worlds, but it is the only one in which the inhabitants have developed a virtual world of their own. The film also involves dreamlike changes in personality and the adoption of other identities. It turns out that Jane herself entered the virtual 1990 version of Los Angeles to assume the role of Fuller's daughter and gain control of the company. Later the consciousness of a bartender, Ashton in the 1937 simulation, takes over the body of one of Hall's associates, Whitney. And Hall turns out to be a virtual incarnation of Jane's real-world husband David. David is killed as Hall in the 1990 simulation and Hall's consciousness takes over David's body in the real world, which turns out to be in 2024. Jane and the real Hannon Fuller are present, and Jane starts to explain to Hall the intricate complexities of the simulations, but as she does so the film ends, with the screen image being reduced to a thin line of light, just like a computer being turned off. Thus yet again a film ends on a note of ambiguity. This time the question is raised: has Hall finally reached the real world, or is he still part of a virtual simulation?

The film *Dreamscape* of 2007 (not to be confused with the 1984 film of the same name), features dreams prominently and bears some comparison with *Total Recall*.

A company called Dreamscape Inc. provides fantastic dreams to its subscribers customised to their requirements while they sleep. A business man commissions a dream about a top secret agent whose mission is to deliver a confidential package. He is hunted down by the state but manages to carry out his mission through brutal means. Gradually the illusion becomes nightmarish and he loses the ability to distinguish between fantasy and reality. The film was reworked and extended and re-released in 2009, but the core remains the same. By contrast with *Inception* the film does not provide much stimulation to reflect on the relationships between dreams and the real waking world.

The main aspect of the film *Sleep Dealer* (2008), directed by Alex Rivera, which it shares with *Inception*, is the use of a technology which enables people to share mental states. It is set in a future world run by a military dictatorship, which utilises the global digital network to control the labour force. The central character, Memo Cruz, works in a factory, as one of the workers who are all connected to the global network via cables joined to nodes in their arms and backs. These workers are known as sleep dealers, and they control robots which have replaced them as skilled physical labourers. A central theme of the film is the contrast between the unreal world of technology and the traditional life of Memo's father as a simple farmer.

The Japanese animé film *Paprika* (2006), co-written and directed by Satoshi Kon, features prominently a procedure enabling people to enter the dreams of others. The purpose of the techonology is to conduct psychotherapeutic treatment. It involves the use of a device called a 'DC Mini'. The head of the research team, Dr. Atsuko Chiba, starts to use the device in an illegal way, to help psychiatric patients outside the research facility. She enters the dream worlds of the patients in her assumed persona of 'Paprika'. However the 'DC minis' have not been fully developed yet with suitable security programs and anyone can steal one and use it to access another's dreams. The story involves much fleeing to and fro from one person's dream into that of another, and the detective Konakawa is pursued into his own recurring dream by a Dr. Osanai, but Konakawa manages to shoot Osanai, thus also killing his own physical body in reality with a real bullet wound. This assumes a different relationship between dreams and reality than that in *Inception*, in which killing someone in a dream results in their returning live and conscious to the real world. In *Paprika* dreams and reality then merge indistinguishably. At the end of the film Konakawa receives a message from Paprika at a website address given to him, telling him to watch a film called *Dreaming Kids*. The possibility is thus left open that the fantasy will continue in some way. The aim of conducting therapeutic treatment by entering the dreams of others is also central to the process of inception, of course, which assumes that it is possible to modify unconscious thoughts via dream encounters in order to change a person's behaviour in the real world.

A Note on Tech-Noir

In the last few decades a new term has come into vogue among film analysts. It is arguable whether it can be said to describe a genre, but it clearly implies a blend of characteristics which can be attributed to some films. It is perhaps fair to describe it as a way of identifying certain kinds of hybrids. In his article, 'Science Fiction – The Last ten Years' in the online journal *YLEM* (2003), Loren Means sums it up succinctly:

> Ten years ago, it appeared that a new film genre was emerging. It was called Tech Noir, after the name of a nightclub in one of the flagship films of the genre, *Terminator*. Tech Noir was something of a hybrid of science fiction and film noir, and its principal examples were *Blade Runner*, *Total Recall*, and three films were manifested in series – *Terminator*, *Alien*, and *Robocop*.[63]

A little later Means adds:

> Tech Noir and Cyberpunk had in common a vision of a 'bad future,' a grungy, hopeless future that promised only greater threats to human life and prosperity than were already the case.[64]

While it is possible to identify elements of sci-fi and film noir in *Inception*, there are clearly no intimations of a '"bad future," a grungy, hopeless future' in the film. The term tech-noir would seem to be applicable in some degree however, if one accepts the validity of Paul Meehan's claim, in his study *Tech Noir, The Fusion of Science Fiction and Film Noir* (2008): 'It should be noted that practically all of science fiction involves some aspect of technology that goes terribly wrong, and is in some sense dark, or noir.'[65] It can be argued that the suspense in *Inception* is maintained by the depiction of a technology (the inception process) which is constantly on the verge of bringing about disaster, but over which human ingenuity ultimately triumphs.

Meehan also points out that the films commonly identified as tech noir freely explore deeper levels of human psychology: 'Tech-noir represents a purely human dimension of the science fiction film, one that casts light on the darker regions of the human heart.'[66]

Another aspect of tech noir which makes it at least partially applicable to *Inception*, is the theme of conflict with powerful conglomerates: 'In tech-noir, wealthy individuals have been replaced by corrupt corporations backed by seemingly limitless money and power.'[67]

5. Dreams and the Cinema

It is perhaps logical to start with the theory that the experience of cinema is akin to that of dreaming, before considering what methods are used in *Inception* to depict the dream states.

Oneiric Film Theory

The term 'oneiric' means simply pertaining to dreams or dreamlike.[68] It is certainly a commonly held belief that films have a dreamlike quality, hence the popular epithet for Hollywood as 'The Dream Factory'. The superficial similarity between experiencing a dream and viewing a film is that in both states the conscious mind is cut off from the outside world and engrossed in a fictive visual dramatisation. A major difference, of course, is that in viewing a film the conscious critical faculties are all operative and one can at any moment distance oneself from the experience and consider extraneous things. In a dream however one is a 'captive audience'. There are nevertheless significant similarities: the camera, like the dreamer, can move in any direction and at any speed and also apparently defy gravity; images can be superimposed on each other and distorted by various technical means; and various forms of metamorphosis are possible, etc. It can be argued, of course, that many viewers of films do not retain sufficient critical distance: they forget the real world around them and outside the cinema and imagine themselves to be part of the action or at least identify to a great extent with leading characters in the drama. They are also only too willing to suspend disbelief and accept as real all manner of unlikely or physically impossible events. Such individuals are particularly suggestive, in the psychological sense. Most viewers of films retain some awareness throughout that they are indeed watching a film. A closer parallel therefore can be drawn between watching a film and that experience, within a dream, of knowing that one is dreaming. This latter state is crucial to an understanding of the process of inception.

Christopher Nolan on Dreaming and Filming

In the documentary material provided with the DVD of *Inception*, Nolan has explained why dreams have interested him. Quotations of his words here have been transcribed from a viewing of the documentary film material. Minor language errors or slips have been omitted or corrected.

Experiencing Dreams

Dreams interest Nolan because they enable ordinary people to experience something akin to unusual mental states:

> ...dreaming is a very positive and healthy experience, and it is one in which somebody [with] normal and ordinary mental process is allowed to view the world in a particularly distorted and surreal way.

One 'very positive and healthy experience' provided in dreams, and which Nolan mentions specifically, is the opportunity to see and talk to people again with whom one has lost contact with or who have died. In *Inception*, Cobb is of course partly motivated by such a desire to see his dead wife again, though also by the need to work through his obsession with her. Nolan himself makes the connection:

> The film certainly deals with the idea that in a dream you can re-experience your time with somebody who has either passed away or is no longer around.

Nolan also stresses that, however bizarre the circumstances in a dream, the emotions experienced are as real as those in waking life, and neither in a dream nor in waking life can we provide evidence for these emotions:

> The emotions of the experiences are real. They're as real as the emotions you experience in the real world. There's no more proof for these things in the real world than there is in the state of the mind. That is where emotion takes place.

For Nolan the experience that humans have of the normal world around them is essentially an illusion. Each individual is trapped within him- or herself, and Nolan believes that the creative person can enable this trapped individual to understand how others view the world:

> ...I think story-telling is one way in which we can understand a different point of
> view on what we consider to be objective reality.

Through presenting distorted views of reality in his films and also by enabling the
audience to identify with characters who experience a distorted view of reality, he
believes he can help others to realise the extent to which they are trapped within
their own illusions:

> What is interesting to me about a film, or characters who either have memory loss
> or distorted perceptions for some reason, is those characters make it immediately
> apparent to the audience that they cannot perceive reality around them. That's true
> of all human beings.

This effect, of temporarily breaking down the sense of there being barriers between
people, provides pleasure for the audience, 'stepping outside the prison of our
perceptions, if only for a brief period of time'.

One of the characteristics of a dream which it shares with a film is, in Nolan's view,
that it breaks up the experience of the real world into fragments, and reassembles
these fragments in a new, surprising and interesting way. In this way the dream is
'a pretty fascinating creative space'. It 'takes the pieces of the real world and mixes
them up into bizarre combinations, by shifting the pieces round'.

Another feature common to both dreams and films, Nolan says, is the way they play
with time. He has always felt that, in his dreams, his brain was working 'faster than
it can do in waking life'. But while his brain may seem to be working faster in his
dreams, time seems to pass more slowly in them: 'I drift off for ten minutes but have
an hour-long dream.' In *Inception* Nolan utilised this experience and extended the
idea beyond what is normally experienced in dreams.

Nolan also admits to having had the experience himself of 'waking' only to find that
he was in another dream. For him this experience reveals the extensiveness of the
mind's creativity: '...that supports this infinite potential of the mind.'

Filming Dreams

Nolan also talks in the DVD interview about the challenges of depicting dream states in film. He realised that verbal accounts of dreams are inadequate and fail to convey the experiences of being in a dream: 'Which is one of the reasons I was interested to make a film that would try and portray dream states.'

It occurred to Nolan that there is one characteristic common to everyone's experience of dreaming: we are aware of waking up from a dream, but never of entering into it. His intention was to enable the audience for his film to experience the dream state in the same way:

> The way we portray the entry into dreams is we throw the audience into the middle of an experience, and then they become oriented through coming out of the dream.

It obviously depends very much on how the transition from one scene to another is handled technically, i.e. how the film is edited. Nolan says that he came to the conclusion that one simple technique of film editing was the most convincing:

> Over the years people tried dissolves, more surreal transitions, but I think the simple cut in film grammar is one of the closest film tricks to the way the brain actually thinks, to the way you actually perceive the world.

In film editing a cut is a direct and immediate transition from one scene into another. Audiences have become used to this mode of transition, and Nolan decided to exploit this fact to the full:

> We've tried to really push the limits of how you can use cuts, how you can use the most simple cinematic transition there is, to take the audience from literally one state of mind into another state of mind.

How *Inception* Uses Dream Theory

From the very beginning of *Inception* the audience is made uncertain whether they are observing a world they should accept as the 'normal' real world, or whether they are inside someone's dream or indeed being presented with a memory in flashback of one of the characters. A bearded man in the surf on a beach seems to see two children building sandcastles on a beach. Is it the same beach? Later events seem to suggest that it is not: the children are Caucasian but soon we learn that the man is in Japan, through the presence of Japanese guards and a view of a Japanese castle. We naturally conclude therefore that the view of the children must be some kind of memory. Then after a sequence between the bearded man and an ancient Japanese man in the castle, we are suddenly transported back to a scene with the same two men when they were much younger. The whole previous sequence would seem therefore to have been some kind of 'flash forward'. Are we now in a 'normal real world'? Whatever the answer to this question may be, the audience continues to observe action in this particular 'reality' for some considerable time. The sequence as a whole can be called, for convenience, the First Heist Plot. It includes a discussion about the nature of 'extraction' and about the nature of the subconscious mind.

For a while, it appears to the audience that they are watching a stage in the narrative prior to immersion in a dream, a planning stage, but then uncertainty arises. Some clues are provided for the audience. It is Cobb who first plants the doubt and, incidentally, makes the first reference to a safe (a recurring image and metaphor) in the film: 'If this is a dream and you have got a safe full of secrets, I need to know what's in that safe.' Saito smiles and leaves, in order to consider their proposal, and Arthur makes a remark which is mysterious to the audience at this stage: 'He knows.' We learn only later that he means that Saito knows they are all in a dream.

Uncertainty is also reinforced for the audience as other scenes are interpolated: a street scene with noisy crowds, Cobb sitting on a chair asleep in some kind of dirty bathroom, other men connected to something and to each other by metal tubes. When Cobb asks Saito if he has known all along, Saito at first interprets this as meaning that he has known that Cobb was planning to steal from him, but quickly adds 'Or that we're actually asleep.' And when Mal threatens to shoot Arthur in the head, Cobb says 'Ah, there's no use threatening him in a dream, right, Mal?' Mal realises the truth of this and wounds Arthur in the leg rather than killing him, which would only wake him up. At this point the significance of Mal identifying the painting by Francis Bacon on the wall in an earlier sequence as being in Arthur's taste becomes clear. She believes they are in Arthur's mind. Cobb promptly kills Arthur to propel him out of this dream into the 'filthy bathroom'.

The dialogue in the bathroom between Arthur and Nash leads the audience to think that this bathroom is indeed the 'real world'. Arthur says '...the dream's collapsing. I'm going to try to keep Saito under a little bit longer.' But then the reality of the scene is put into doubt by the insertion of a scene in a Japanese bullet train. Both Nash and Arthur are asleep on the train. A Japanese man, Todashi, opens a metal brief case containing a mechanism and an MP3 player. He plays music into Nash's headphones. It is the first time for us to hear the song, Edith Piaf's 'Non, Je ne regrette rien', which is to feature in the film as the 'kick', transferring people from the dream state into the waking state.

Confirmation that they are now in a dream within a dream comes from Saito himself. He laughs when he notices that the carpet in the room is not made from the same material as that in the real room he had been using as a 'love nest'. Saito is now impressed with Cobb's accomplishment: 'You've lived up to your reputation, Mr. Cobb... I'm still dreaming.' What Saito had not realised, however, is that this dream within a dream is not in his own mind. Before vanishing Cobb informs him 'We're not in your dream.' Nash enlightens him: 'We're in mine.' When Saito eventually wakes in the bullet train he find himself in the bullet train alone with Todashi, who is reading a comic. He rubs a patch on his wrist, presumably where the tube was connected, and smiles. We can deduce that he is recalling events in the dream states he has experienced.

At this point it is useful to review the nature of the dream states depicted so far in the film and consider the presuppositions about the nature of dreams and the subconscious mind.

The Subconscious and Extraction

It is clear that the film assumes the existence of an unconscious area of the mind (what Cobb refers to as the 'subconscious'), which can be influenced through access by skilled operators: '...we can train your subconscious to defend itself from even the most skilled extractor.' While explaining extraction to Saito early in the film, Cobb speaks of ideas in the brain which cannot be eradicated. He asserts that an idea is 'the most resilient parasite'. And this is very much in accordance with Freud's concept of repression: disturbing thoughts are repressed from consciousness, but, if such thoughts, or ideas, are *too* disturbing they start to force their way back into consciousness, and the sleeping mind distorts them, changes them in some way, so that they can be contemplated in dreams but will not break through into consciousness. Extraction is a process of gaining access to such a repressed idea. A sci-fi element is introduced in the film, with the notion that it is possible to train the subconscious to defend itself against extraction.

Dreams within Dreams

Another feature of the dream experience which is introduced during the First Heist Plot is that it is sometimes possible to be aware, while one is dreaming, that one is dreaming. In *Inception* such awareness becomes problematic, as when Saito starts to realise that what is happening in the Japanese castle may be part of a dream, and that the mind of the dreamer can escape into another dream, rather than wake up. This is in accordance with Freud's explanation of the phenomenon. For Freud the experience of coming out of one dream only to find onself in another is further evidence that the process of censorship is at work again. Some details of the original dream which are disturbing and unacceptable to the dreamer are becoming too clear and can be identified easily. They thus become subjected to further censorship. By 'waking' into another dream, the mind is telling itself that there is no need to wake up, as it is all just a dream. It is then possible to 'wake' yet again from this dream within a dream:

> The intention is… to detract from the importance of what is 'dreamt' in the dream, to rob it of its reality. What is dreamt in a dream after waking from the 'dream within a dream' is what the dream-work seeks to put in the place of an obliterated reality.[69]

It will be seen later that a similar mechanism is at work in the 'Mr. Charles' gambit employed by Cobb.

Extraneous Disturbance

Arthur experiences a disturbance

Another characteristic of dreams which is utilised in these opening sequences of the film and which will feature later on many occasions, is the way in which forces extraneous to the dream state, but which impinge upon it, are interpreted by the sleeping mind. Such forces are interpreted by the sleeping mind in ways which enable them to be incorporated into the dream narrative, without causing the dreamer to wake up. This is explained further in the DVD documentary accompanying the film by Prof. G. William Domhoff. In the film it is also assumed that disturbing forces in one level of dreaming are similarly incorporated into the next level of dreaming, into the dream within a dream. In the First Heist sequence of the film such disturbances are hinted at but not explained, e.g. while Cobb is explaining extraction to Saito, a tremor occurs and items on a table shake. Arthur provides the hint that there is another level of consciousness when he asks at this juncture, 'What's going on up there?' Then when the scene does change to another level, the 'filthy bathroom', there are several unexplained disturbances from outside the building, suggesting disruptive forces: a brief shot of a street scene with rioting, crowds, cars and fires. A little later there is a shot of a car exploding into flames outside. Another example of hints, which are at the time not explained, is the way in which the Japanese castle becomes rapidly swamped with water. Later, in the first level of the inception dream, Yusuf's physical need to urinate, essentially something extraneous to the dream state, manifests itself in the dream as heavy rain, and Cobb, aware of its significance, makes a joke of it. And in the hotel lobby sequence in the second level of the inception dream, the bad weather in the first level starts to disrupt the stability of the building. Extraneous disturbance is used positively of course in the form of the musical cue (the Piaf song), which functions as the 'kick', to bring the team out of the dream state once and for all.

The Prime Dreamer

One notion that Nolan is concerned to remind the audience of throughout the dream is that at each stage of inception there is always a prime dreamer. The dream state is never assumed to exist independently, i.e. it is not an artificially created medium in which all of the team participate, merging their own individual consciousness into an independently existing virtual world. A dream presupposes a dreamer and the others participate in his/her dream. Thus the sequence in Saito's 'love-nest' when he discovers it is not real is part of Nash's dream. When Ariadne is demonstrating her skills as an architectural designer to Cobb, we are in her dream. And of course Ariadne enters into Cobb's dream to find out what he is investigating at night. When the team begins the inception process and enters into the first level, it is, as we have seen, Yusuf's dream. Yusuf then remains in charge of the mechanism at that level, when the team descend to the second level, in the hotel, where Arthur is the prime dreamer, and must remain there when the descent is made to the third level, to ensure that the sleeping team can be returned later to the waking state. In the third level, the snowy mountains with fortified hospital complex, the prime dreamer is Eames. In dialogue on the mountains Cobb makes this clear: 'Eames, this is your dream. I need you to draw the security away from the complex, understand?'

It should be noted that this notion of a prime dreamer is an example of science fiction being in accordance with scientific fact. Neuroscientific research has shown that there is always an identifiable entity, the self, at the centre of a dream. J. Allan Hobson has stressed that the identity of the dreamer is never in doubt:

> ...the only dimension of orientation that is secure in dreaming is the sense of self – I am always at the centre of the vortex that is my dream.[70]

Concurrent Dreams

One of the most questionable notions in the film is that of concurrent dreams. It is a prime supposition which enables the interaction of three storylines: the sequence with Yusuf in the van, the sequence with Arthur in the hotel, and the sequence with Eames on the mountains. While this is acceptable as a device in film-making for pursuing three interrelated storylines, there is no evidence that it is possible in the actual state of dreaming. In the state of a 'dream within a dream' one dream is *relinquished* and another dream takes its place. Suspension of disbelief is required for this aspect of the film, as is also required for how the mechanism actually functions (it is never explained). It would appear to be a 'real' mechanism in the 747 sequence, in which the inception process is initiated, but henceforth it is a 'dreamed' mechanism, i.e. it is recreated in the mind of the particular prime dreamer. If it is no longer a 'real' mechanism, how can it effect real change, i.e. bring about descent to another level? And how can it exist concurrently in the 747, in the van and in the hotel room?

Some important facets of the dreams in *Inception* can be convincingly explained with Freudian and Jungian terminology. There follows examples of such explanations with reference to the relevant concepts: projection, condensation, displacement, symbolism and archetypes.

Projection

Projection is a term used frequently in the film, with little explanation provided of its psychological significance. We are informed on several occasions that certain figures in the film are projections by one of the characters. It is important to note that in the film they are mainly presented as defence mechanisms, personifications created by the dreamer's mind. They become aggressive at any disturbing influences from other selves intruding from outside the dreamer's mind, such as the members of the team conducting inception. This is one specific usage of a term which has wider applications in theoretical psychology.

The analytic psychologist C. G. Jung regarded projection as a normal aspect of the way we view and interpret the world and other human beings. His definition in *General Aspects of Dream Psychology* is lengthy but useful:

> Just as we tend to assume that the world is as we see it, we naïvely suppose that people are as we imagine them to be. In this latter case, unfortunately, there is no scientific test that would prove the discrepancy between perception and reality. Although the possibility of gross deception is infinitely greater here than in our perception of the physical world, we still go on naïvely projecting our own psychology into our fellow human beings. In this way everyone creates for himself a series of more or less imaginary relationships based essentially on projection.[71]

And as in anxious waking life so also in the case of dreams: '...all the figures in the dream are personified features of the dreamer's own personality.'[72]

Jung draws an illuminating comparison of the mind when in a state of dreaming with the experience of a play in a theatre. It takes only a little imagination to perceive that the metaphor can easily be modified to apply to film-making, and the dreamer considered to be the 'auteur' of his or her dream: 'The whole dream-work is essentially subjective, and the dream is a theatre in which the dreamer is himself the scene, the player, the prompter, the producer, the author, the public, and the critic.'[73] Thus it should be remembered that basically everything experienced in a dream is in some way a projection of the dreamer's mind. In *Inception*, however, the dreams are not naturally occurring ones but have been induced and the settings artificially designed by Ariadne. Projection is thus limited to the other human figures who appear.

It may not be clear to the audience of the film on first viewing, but all the guards and armed paramilitary figures in the film are projections of the subject of the dream, of the 'mark', whether it be for extraction (Saito) or for inception (Robert Fischer). Thus the Japanese guards in the opening sequence are projections of Saito, defending the secret that Cobb is trying to steal. A projection of Cobb's, namely Mal, interferes with this process. Mal is very complex as a projection and will be examined subsequently.

We learn from Arthur, through his explanation to Saito, that in a natural state of dreaming the dreamer is not always able to defend himself from intrusions from without: in a dream state defences are lowered and ideas can be extracted. But Cobb offers to help Saito protect himself against such intrusion by training his projections to function as guards. It becomes clear later, of course, that Cobb is conducting a double bluff here: his offer is a way of gaining access. Cobb says that it will only work if Saito lowers his defences, so that he, Cobb, can access his mind, learn his scerets, and so help him establish his own defences. He says to Saito: '...we can train your subconscious to defend itself from even the most skilled extractor.' This is the first use of the term 'subconscious' in the film. It is used in the film to refer to the whole realm of the mind not directly accessible to normal consciousness. Freud and Jung preferred to call this the 'unconscious'.

It becomes clear that the reason why it is necessary to design very complex architecture, like mazes, for the dream states to be used in inception, is to make it difficult for the projections, both Fischer's guards and Cobb's projection of Mal, to gain access to the team and to disrupt the process of inception. We have the first hint of this during Cobb's conversation with Miles in a lecture hall. Regarding Cobb's need for someone to design the dream architecture, Miles first suggests 'Design it yourself', but Cobb replies 'Mal won't let me.'

During a sequence in which Cobb is training Ariadne and they are walking together inside a dream in a Paris street designed by her, Cobb explains to her the relationship between the dreamer, that is the subject of inception, and the projections. The people, he says, are projections of his subconscious (as the subject): '...you are the dreamer. You built this world. I am the subject. My mind populates it. That's one of the ways we extract information from the subject.' As they walk farther along the street, the projections of people around them become more aggressive in manner towards Ariadne. As projections of Cobb's subconscious they are concerned to defend his interests. Ariadne notices more and more that the other people are looking at her directly. The projections are essentially becoming 'aware' that some external agency is modifying the world they inhabit. In Cobb's words, they are looking at Ariadne 'because my subconscious *feels* that someone else is creating this world. The more you change things, the quicker the projections converge on you.' He describes their

A variety of 'projections' at different dream state levels

defensive function using a physiological metaphor: 'They sense the foreign nature of the dreamer. They attack – like white blood cells fighting an infection.' They eventually come to a bridge and the projections start to become more aggressive towards Ariadne, who says 'Mind telling your subconscious to take it easy?' And we learn another fact about these subconscious projections: they are not under the subject's control. Cobb explains: 'It's my *sub*conscious. Remember, I don't control it.'

The climax of this particular dream sequence, in which Mal appears and attempts to attack Ariadne, is brought about because Ariadne has used elements of real memory in her reconstruction, a whole bridge in Paris which is familiar to her. It is also familiar to Cobb and awakens a memory of Mal. His projection of Mal can thus gain access to him via associated memories. This is why he tells Ariadne: 'Never recreate places from your memory. Always imagine new places.' And he adds: 'Only use details – a streetlamp, or a phone booth, never whole areas.' As Mal materialises and marches towards Ariadne, the other figures, as Cobb's projections, become more defensive. It is significant that they attack Ariadne and not Mal. This can be explained by the fact that Ariadne has started to guess the truth that Cobb is trying to conceal. Mal and the other projections attempt to silence her.

In a later scene, while Arthur is explaining to Ariadne the nature of the paradoxical architecture they must construct for their dream sequences, he also reiterates and clarifies for her (and thus for the audience, should it still be confused!) why the architecture must be a complex maze-like structure. It is, of course, to provide defence against attack from the projections. Arthur is at this stage the only member of the team who knows about Cobb's problems with Mal. He explains to Ariadne that although the projections of many people may not be especially aggressive, they can become so if they sense hostile intruders. 'You wait, they'll turn ugly. No one likes to feel someone else messing around in their mind.' And he makes clear to her that this is why Cobb prefers not to know the layout, because his own projection of Mal is getting stronger. Ariadne, and thus the audience, learn for the first time at this point, that Mal is Cobb's dead wife. The fact that Cobb's projection of Mal is getting stronger implies that he is becoming less and less able to repress his unresolved guilt complex related to her. This is confirmed very shortly after this sequence when Cobb tries out the drug in Yusuf's pharmacy and experiences a very vivid image of Mal telling him 'You know what you have to do.'

The next powerful manifestation of aggressive projections occurs just after the entry into the level one dream (the car chase in city streets in heavy rain). The team is pursued by a vehicle with men shooting at them. The audience learn only later that these are members of Fischer's 'sub-security' attempting to defend him.

In the second level of the dream, when Cobb decides to employ the 'Mr. Charles gambit', the other people in the bar, projections by Fischer, suddenly start to become aggressive. One reason for the rise in aggression is that, as Arthur explains to Ariadne, the function of the 'Mr. Charles gambit' is to turn Fischer against his own subconscious. As the subject becomes aware of the fact that he is in a dream, then the sub-security also becomes aware that there are unfamiliar figures in the dream, intruders who might have bad intentions. In confirmation of this there is a brief sequence shortly afterwards in which Saito is pursued by sub-security men. He disposes of Fischer's wallet, which has come into his possession, in a waste chute. The main focus of the bar guests' aggression is, however, on Arthur, because he is the prime dreamer at this level. The culmination of the 'Mr. Charles gambit' is the gunfight in the washroom between Cobb and two of the sub-security men, whom he manages to kill. He reinterprets their role to gain Fischer's trust. He manages to persuade Fischer that these men were not there to protect him: 'These men were sent to abduct you.'

The final manifestation of aggressive projections is in the third level dream state, in and around the fortified mountain hospital complex. Because Eames is the prime dreamer at this level, Cobb instructs him to provoke the militarised guards to draw their attention away from Cobb and Ariadne. The denouement of the conflict between Cobb and his projection of Mal will be examined in due course.

Condensation

Condensation is an important concept in psychoanalytic thought. For Freud the mind constantly seeks the most economical means of expression. In defining condensation he distinguishes between the dream as recalled and the dream as experienced together with its explication. The dreams as recalled by the dreamer he calls the manifest dream; the detailed account of the meaning of the dream taking into account the censored thoughts is the latent dream: 'The first achievement of the dream-work is *condensation*. By that we understand the fact that the manifest dream has a smaller content than the latent one, and is thus an abbreviated translation of it.'[74] Omission and fragmentation take place, and especially interesting for an analysis of the film is the fact that several elements are often combined into one. Freud reminded the audience of his lectures that they could all certainly recall examples of such fusion, of 'different people being condensed into a single one'.[75]

Notable examples of such condensation in *Inception* are Eames' adoptions of the appearances of two people, Browning (Tom Berenger) and the blonde woman in the bar.

Eames and Browning

Eames' skills in forgery and deception are established during our first encounter with him in the film. When Eames impersonates Browning it is not achieved by clever make-up or by some magical substitution: he has first to study Browning's character and his relationship with both Robert Fischer and Fischer's father. Thus, in conversation with Saito, Eames takes the opportunity to quiz him about Fischer's relationship with his father. As Saito can only provide vague information Eames suggests that Saito arrange a meeting between himself and Browning, 'Fischer's senior right-hand, Fischer junior's godfather'. We then cut to two scenes with Robert Browning, in which Eames is also present. Browning is discussing the question of litigation with a lawyer. Eames watches closely as Browning goes into Maurice Fischer's inner office, which has been adapted to function also as a hospital room. We can deduce that the old man in the bed is Fischer senior and that the younger man by the window is his son Robert. Browning is seen to be concerned about obtaining the power of attorney, and although Robert clearly implies that it is not an appropriate moment to discuss such a matter, he nevertheless reveals how close he is on a personal level to Browning, when he says 'Not now, Uncle Peter.' From this encounter Eames perceives how important it is to weaken the power of Browning.

Eames changing into Browning

In voice-over he says 'the sicker Maurice Fischer becomes, the stronger Peter Browning becomes...'. In subsequent scenes Eames explains how his plan to impersonate Browning will work. We see his face reflected back in a mirror, like the kind used by actors in their dressing rooms, as Browning. It is the kind of condensation of persons that Freud identified in the dream work. Eames will set about his task in the following way: 'Now, in the first layer of the dream, I can impersonate Browning and suggest concepts to Fischer's conscious mind.' His supposition is then that they will be able to take Fischer down another level of dreaming, i.e. into a dream within a dream, 'and his own projection should feed it right back to him'. Then he explains further: 'That's the only way it will stick. It has to seem *self-generated*.'

In the actual process of inception when Eames impersonates Browning, it is made clear that it involves the kind of condensation that can only occur in dreams by having the role played by the actual actor who played Browning earlier and not a made-up Eames. In a later scene when Fischer confronts Browning there is a danger of the audience becoming confused as to whether this Browning is really Eames or Fischer's projection of Browning (in accordance with Eames' prediction that 'his own projection should feed it right back to him'). To avoid this confusion there is a brief scene, which is not without a touch of humour, involving mistaken identity: we see

Saito in the lobby with Browning coming towards him. He clearly thinks it is still Eames in disguise, saying 'I see you've changed.' But then Eames appears as himself behind Browning, and Saito has to apologise: 'Oh, I'm sorry... I mistook you for a friend.' So who is this Browning in a dream within a dream? Eames enlightens Saito: 'That's Fischer's projection of Browning.' He suggests that they follow him to observe if Fischer is starting to suspect Browning's motives as they want him to.

We are then in Room 528. Someone lets themselves into the room with a key. It is Browning, whom Arthur promptly throws to the floor, putting a gun to his head. Cobb reveals that Browning has a key with the number 528 on it. How did the team contrive for him to have this number on the key? The answer must be that they did not. As Browning is here a projection of Fischer's, it must be Fischer's growing suspicion of his godfather's motives which has furnished the number: his subconscious is beginning to suspect. Cobb feeds this suspicion, making Fischer aware of the fact that he and Browning were not kidnapped together. When Fischer says that Browning was being tortured, Cobb also throws into doubt Fischer's evidence: 'You saw them torture him?' He now suspects that it is Browning's intention to open the safe, 'to get the alternate will'. It must be borne in mind that the ensuing conversation between Fischer and Browning is engendered by Fischer's own subconscious, so that Browning should be understood to be voicing what Fischer suspects Browning of thinking. Browning says he wants to prevent Robert from rising 'to your father's last taunt'. He tries to persuade Robert that the will in question is 'his last insult'. It is 'a challenge for you to build something for yourself, by telling you you're not worthy of his accomplishments'. Fischer now takes this to be the sense of his father's last word to him: 'Disappointed.' Browning appears to be wanting Robert to ignore his father's apparent 'last will' and instead to reinforce the present company: 'I'm sorry. But he's wrong. You can build a better company than he ever did.' But shortly before describing his father's alternate will as a taunt, Browning had said: 'Fischer Morrow's been my entire life. I can't let you destroy it.' Cobb reinforces Fischer's growing suspicion by telling him that Browning is lying, and reassures him by adding: 'Trust me. It's what I do. He's hiding something, and we need to find out what that is,' at which point Eames and Saito enter. This is the cue to undertake the transition to the third level of the dream.

Eames and the Blonde Woman

Eames changing into blonde woman

There is another 'cameo performance' by Eames, demonstrating his versatility in impersonation. This time it is as the blonde woman in the bar, and it is another example of condensation. In order to perform the 'Mr. Charles gambit' Cobb will need something to distract both Fischer and his watching sub-security in the hotel lobby bar, and Eames offers to perform another of his impersonations: 'How about a lovely lady that I've used before?' After his calling Arthur 'Darling' one cannot help wondering if there might be a camp side to Eames' nature, a gender instability which enables him psychologically to assume other personalities easily.

Immediately after entry into the level two dream, in a hotel lobby bar, the blonde woman makes her first appearance. We are in the middle of a conversation between Fischer and this beautiful blonde, who is telling him about herself. The audience may already have guessed that this is Eames in another of his guises, but it is not yet made explicit. When Cobb approaches Fischer and commences the 'Mr. Charles gambit', the blonde leaves them, putting a napkin in front of Fischer. Members of the sub-security follow her. She thus fulfils her function as a distraction. Cobb draws Fischer's attention to what is apparently her six-digit phone number which she has written on the napkin. It is: 528-491. This is, of course, exactly the same sequence of numbers that Fischer had come up with, spontaneously, when pressed to choose a sequence for the combination of the safe. One must assume that this is part of the plan to fix the number in Fischer's mind. Eames, now the blonde, must have heard it as Browning while tied up next to Fischer in the interrogation scene.

Cobb now draws Fischer's attention to the fact that the blonde has stolen his wallet (pick-pocketing being a skill that Eames has demonstrated already on the plane when he obtained Fischer's passport). Fischer is concerned because it is a valuable wallet, but Cobb reassures him, letting slip, deliberately one assumes, as he does so, the fact that he has some connection with security: 'Don't worry about it. My people are on it as we speak.'

There then occurs a short sequence between Saito and the blonde, as Saito attempts to come out of a lift, elsewhere in the hotel. The blonde pushes him back into the lift and moves close to him. Saito can see their reflections over the blonde's shoulder, in what the shooting script describes as 'the tunnel of infinite reflections created by the elevator's opposing mirrors' (shooting script p.152), and the blonde is revealed to be Eames. Having now changed to his normal appearance, Eames takes out Fischer's wallet and looks at the photo in it of Fischer and his father. The use of mirrors again, as when Eames adopts the character of Browning, serves to emphasise that the Eames/blonde woman figure is a dream-like condensation and not just Eames in convincing make-up.

Displacement

Another Freudian concept can be adduced to explain an especially strange feature of the film, and which lends it at times a bizarre quality. The term in German is *Verschiebung*, which is usually translated as *displacement*.

Displacement is essentially a strategy adopted in the censorship process of the dream-work to divert the focus of interest away from one idea to another, so that the first idea loses its power to disturb. Freud describes it thus:

It manifests itself in two ways: in the first, a latent element is replaced not by a component part of itself but by something more remote – that is, by an allusion; and in the second, the psychical accent is shifted from an important element on to another which is unimportant, so that the dream appears differently centred and strange.[76]

Displacement is successful only if it manages to divert the mind away from the original latent thought completely:

> ...the dream-censorship only gains its end if it succeeds in making it impossible to find a path back from the allusion to the genuine thing.[77]

The allusions employed for the purposes of displacement in dreams '...are connected with the element they replace by the most external and remote relations and are therefore unintelligible...'.[78] In *Inception* one of the most memorable examples of such displacement in the dreams is the recurrence of various images of trains and railways. At first this is mystifying, intentionally so, but gradually the viewer discovers that such images are allusions to Cobb's wife Mal. His complex of unresolved feelings concerning her is trying to enter into his consciousness.

The first reference to trains and railways in the film, which links this image to Cobb's relationship with Mal, occurs when Cobb decides to try out for himself the effects of the drug in Yosuf's pharmacy. It will be recalled that there is a close up of a railway line with the sound of an approaching train, and Cobb and Mal are lying with their faces against one of the rails. The next allusion to trains occurs briefly during the sequence when Ariadne intrudes into Cobb's experiment with his own dreams. She travels between the different levels of his dream state in a lift which has a cage-like structure. After a fraught meeting with Mal and discussion with Cobb, she manages to escape into the lift again, slams the door shut and presses a button to make the lift descend. We see various other levels in passing, including Mal's childhood bedroom, and a sudden startling close-up of some kind of freight train rushing past. As we are in Cobb's dream this latter image is clearly an allusion to the sequence we have seen earlier with Cobb and Mal lying on a railway line, and a reminder, through its association with Mal, of the disturbing influence of Cobb's memory of her.

The first clear example of the railway image functioning as a disturbing element in the inception process occurs in the car chase through rainy streets, just after entering the level one dream. Again it is clear displacement for Cobb's unresolved complex involving Mal. We see Cobb's car being blocked by another car, which in turn is hit by a huge freight train appearing out of nowhere, which also cuts Cobb's car off from the cab. Ariadne watches the passing freight train and clearly begins to suspect that something is amiss: 'This wasn't in the design.' Finally Cobb manages to get round the end of the train, which has been blocking their way.

In a later discussion between Cobb and Ariadne she reveals that she now understands the significance of the train image. She reminds him that the rest of the team do not know the truth about him that she now knows:

> The truth that at any minute you might bring a freight train through the wall. The truth that Mal is bursting up through your subconscious. the truth that as we go deeper into Fischer, we're also going deeper into you – and I'm not sure we're going to like what we find.

The train image is associated with Cobb's promise that he and Mal would stay together throughout their whole lives. The riddle that Mal tells Ariadne is of a never-ending train journey, and whenever there is an allusion to it, it is a reminder to Cobb of the promise that he failed to fulfil.

There are two other minor examples of displacement in the film, which also allude only indirectly to Cobb's sense of guilt about Mal. While Cobb is conducting the 'Mr. Charles gambit' in the lobby, a waiter tips over and smashes a champagne glass. This provides a link in Cobb's memory with the sequence in a hotel suite with Mal on the occasion of their anniversary, when a champagne glass is broken, and Ariadne also steps on a broken champagne glass when she accesses such a suite in Cobb's dream. In the sequence during the 'Mr. Charles gambit' the association with Mal is clearly stimulated by the waiter's accident, because immediately afterwards Cobb glimpses his two children crouched with their backs towards the camera in another part of the lobby. It all indicates that his guilt complex is starting to disturb his consciousness again. The occasional images of billowing white curtains in a window can also be considered as examples of such displacement, alluding to the scene in the anniversary suite again. One notable example occurs when Cobb drops off to sleep before entering the third level of the dream: we catch the briefest glimpse of billowing white curtains again.

Symbolism

Symbolism as it occurs in dreams is to be understood as serving different functions to those in creative writing and art, although similarities can be identified. The theories of Freud and Jung again provide the foundations of the modern usage in a psychological sense.

It is important to deal straight away with a common misapprehension about Freud's theory of symbolism in dreams. He did not believe that certain objects and images in dreams have a fixed meaning and that whenever they occur in any dream they have the same meaning. He criticised previous dream theories for this very fault. He did, however, believe that certain objects and images lend themselves naturally to express certain things. Thus upright objects lend themselves easily to allusions to the phallus. But sometimes a pole is just a pole and does not automatically signify a phallus. In the *Introductory Lectures* he describes the process of symbolisation as follows:

> It consists in transforming thoughts into visual images. Let us keep it clear that this transformation does not affect *everything* in the dream-thoughts; some of them retain their form and appearance as thoughts or knowledge in the manifest dream as well...[79]

However, once a latent thought has been 'translated' into a symbol, the object selected as such a symbol retains its significance as such throughout the particular dream:

> A constant relation... between a dream-element and its translation is described by us as a 'symbolic' one, and the dream-element itself as a 'symbol' of the unconscious dream-thought.[80]

One clear example of such a symbol in *Inception* is that of the safe, in which information can be 'locked away' in deep recesses of the mind. This symbol occurs in the extraction sequence in the Japanese castle, in Mal's bedroom and in the locked room in the snowbound mountain hospital at the climax of the film.

Freud was very much aware that he was using the term symbol in only a loosely and not clearly defined way:

A locked safe appears at several crucial junctures throughout the film

> We must admit, too, that the concept of a symbol cannot at present be
> sharply delimited: it shades off into such notions as those of a replacement or
> representation, and even approaches that of an allusion.[81]

Jung's notion of symbolism is somewhat different to Freud's and is useful in
understanding a different kind of dream symbol as employed in the film. For Jung
'...many dreams present images and associations that are analogous to primitive
ideas, myths, and rites'.[82] The 'images and associations', that Jung finds analogous to
primitive ideas, occur, according to him, as symbols, which for him have a broader
significance than they do for Freud: '...dream symbols are the essential message
carriers from the instinctive to the rational parts of the human mind...'.[83] For Jung
a symbol does not refer back to repressed memories but 'hints at something not
yet known'.[84] We can learn from it: '...the symbol in the dream has more the value
of a parable: it does not conceal, it teaches.'[85] He concurs with Freud, however,
in the belief that dream symbols should not be freely interpreted by the analyst
without reference to the individual character of the dreamer: 'No dream symbol
can be separated from the individual who dreams it, and there is no definite or
straightforward interpretation of any dream.'[86]

One fascinating symbol in *Inception* which is never clearly explained is that of the
child's toy windmill. It features first in the photograph of Fischer with his father, which
is kept by the old man's bedside, and it also appears in the safe together with a
document, which we can assume to be the alternative will. The windmill is clearly
associated with childhood and, as it appears in the photograph, must have actually
existed. It appears to allude to a period when there existed a closer relationship
between Fischer and his father, when they could share playful things. This was lost
in the course of his growing up. Its reappearance in the safe in the culminating
sequence of the third level dream state suggests that Fischer, as the idea planted
by inception takes root, feels reconciled to his father again at least. The childhood
intimacy is re-established. Dreams are purposive, according to Jung, and part of this
purpose is certainly compensation, in the sense of restoring an imbalance in the state
of the mind and warning us if some of our ways of thinking and feeling are likely
to have a negative or destructive effect. In this way they function not as mental
aberrations but as a normal, restorative function of the mind:

...dreams serve the purpose of compensation. This assumption means that the dream is a normal psychic phenomenon that transmits unconscious reactions or spontaneous impulses to consciousness.[87]

So perhaps the very mysteriousness of the toy windmill symbol makes it possible to perceive it as serving to show Fischer the way forward in his personal development, and, in a Jungian sense, it 'hints at something not yet known'. In referring back to Fischer's childhood, it simultaneously alludes to further possibilities and remains ultimately uninterpretable to anyone but the dreamer himself. Parallels might be drawn with the enigmatic image of 'Rosebud' at the end of Orson Welles' film *Citizen Kane* (1941).

The mystery of the toy windmill

Archetypes

Jung believed that everybody shares what he called 'aboriginal, innate, and inherited shapes of the human mind'.[88] These were 'collective images' and 'mythological motifs'[89] to which he applied the term archetypes. In *Psychological Types* (1921), Jung defines archetypes further as 'the accumulated experiences of organic life in general, a million times repeated, and condensed into types'.[90] They are clearly part of a collective unconscious, for they are '...common to entire peoples or epochs. In all probability the most important mythological motifs are common to all times and races...'[91] In dreams thoughts and emotions can be expressed in the form of symbols derived from such archetypes (the 'archetypal treatment of ideas in dreams'[92]). For Jung, archetypes possess an emotional charge and therefore exert a powerful influence in our minds: 'They are, at the same time, both images and emotions. One can speak of an archetype only when these two aspects are simultaneous.'[93] And he adds subsequently: '...by being charged with emotion... it becomes dynamic, and consequences of some kind must flow from it.'[94]

There are many archetypes posited by Jung. Among them are the Child, the Family, the Father, the Mother, the God, the Hero, the Masculine, the Feminine, the Wise Man, etc. Particularly relevant to a study of *Inception* are those of the Anima (a man's perception of the female) and the Animus (a woman's perception of the male). The figure of Mal, Cobb's dead wife, in *Inception*, can be interpreted as an embodiment of the anima archetype.

In life, Mal embodied all the qualities of the feminine, which enabled Cobb to fall in love with her and father her children. When he conducted an experiment in inception on her, she lost the ability to distinguish between what was real and what existed only in the dream worlds they had created. It is a characteristic of the individual dreams in *Inception* that when a participant in the dream state dies, he/she returns then to the real world of normal consciousness. This is why Mal, unable to recognise that she is already in the normal world, commits suicide and encourages Cobb to do likewise. From that moment Cobb is obsessed with his sense of guilt for having brought about this state of mind in Mal. In order to continue actively in his conscious life, the jobs he has to undertake, Cobb has to repress his guilt complex relating to Mal deep within his unconscious. The ideal woman he had loved thus becomes associated with the negative side of his own personality (or his 'shadow' self, another Jungian archetype), and he perceives only the dark destructive side of her personality. This is how Cobb's projection of Mal in the film has acquired destructive qualities. It is in accordance with the perception, in Jungian psychology, that the anima has both positive and negative aspects, as do all archetypes: they have both light and dark aspects. They can bring about positive creative development to the personality, or they can be destructive and bring about the physical death of the person. If the relationship with the anima develops into an unresolved obsession, then the man cannot break free. The negatively charged anima starts to invade consciousness and the man is in a state of being possessed by his anima, which then functions as a mediator between his conscious self and his unconscious. It is from Cobb's determined repression that Mal acquires her strength.

6. Cobb's 'Emotional Journey': From Guilt to Redemption

At the beginning of the section on genre it was pointed out that Nolan felt it was crucial to chart the development of Cobb's character in the film, what he called his 'emotional journey'. In this section his development will be analysed, revealing how he progresses from a haunted, guilt-ridden man through the major part of the film to becoming a man who has come to terms with what he has done and who has redeemed himself morally.

The first shot of Cobb which we see in the film is ambiguous. In fact, we do not know yet who this bearded man is, who has been washed ashore on a beach. And when he then appears to see a boy and a girl on a beach with a sandcastle being destroyed by the tide, we also do not know if he is witnessing this scene at that moment, or whether it is a memory. It becomes obvious after a while that it must be a memory, however, and its recurrence suggests that the children are of some concern to the man. We learn later that this memory indeed is central to Cobb's prime concern in the film: the welfare of his children. It is possible to perceive in the image of the tide destroying the fragile edifice of a sandcastle a metaphor for his anxieties for them.

If the opening sequence encourages some sympathy for Cobb, then the subsequent sequence in which he explains the notion of extraction to Saito provides no further support for this feeling, but presents him rather as a hard-nosed entrepreneur who has a unique service to offer: he can enter another's mind and steal its secrets. And he is willing to break the law if necessary.

The first hint that there is some unresolved emotional conflict in Cobb's mind comes with the first appearance of Mal. The audience does not know at this stage who she is. There are allusions in the dialogue, which only become clear later in the film. She asks 'If I jumped, would I survive?' And a little later she says 'I thought you might be missing me.' Cobb responds with 'You know that I am. But I can't trust you anymore.' We learn later that the reason she is not to be trusted is that she is an image created from his own unconscious, and by their nature such images, being inaccessible to conscious control, should be treated with suspicion. We can guess at this early stage in the film, however, that some kind of guilt complex is causing Cobb to project this image of Mal.

The dialogue continues but the scene changes to a bedroom suite in the Japanese castle. Mal sips champagne, which is of course an allusion forward, a foreshadowing of the scene in their anniversary suite and the sequence when Mal commits suicide (because she believes it is the only way to escape from what she is convinced is a dream, but which is in fact normal waking reality). In this early sequence in the Japanese castle Mal, as a projection of Cobb's unconscious, is thus drawing his mind back to the scene in which his guilt is rooted.

Cobb attempts to fight against the intrusion of this guilt complex, so that he can continue with his extraction. In a dream he can, of course, only do this symbolically. He dons black gloves and puts Mal into a chair. He then ties the chair to a length of rope, goes to the window, and after telling her 'Stay where you are, Mal' he goes out of the window and rappels down the rope. The strength of the disturbing force of Cobb's guilt complex is revealed by the fact that this gambit does not work. Mal must clearly have somehow got out of the chair, because we see it slide empty towards the window and wedge under it.

Mal returns shortly with a vengeance. While Cobb is retrieving the envelope from the safe he has opened, the lights suddenly come on, and Saito appears, in the company of Mal, who now has a gun. This is the climax of the action in the First Heist Plot, and Mal appears determined to disrupt it. In other words Cobb's focus of attention is being disturbed again by his guilt complex. Mal, believing that they are in Arthur's dream, threatens to kill the latter, presumably as a way of blackmailing Cobb to yield to her wishes. When she wounds him instead, Cobb promptly kills Arthur himself, to propel him out of the dream. The whole sequence reveals how repressed guilt feelings can express themselves in violent ways if left unresolved.

After Saito has guessed that they have been in a dream within a dream, and when the film cuts to the bullet train, we learn that Cobb is planning to get off the train at Kyoto. Arthur realises that one reason at least for this is to avoid Saito when they finally wake him up: 'He's not gonna check every compartment.' Cobb's reply may be superficially like a joke, but it also reflects genuine anxiety, which is linked to a recurring disruptive image in the film: 'Yeah, well, I don't like trains.'

Shortly after this we see Cobb looking weary and sitting in an apartment, which is identified in the shooting script as being in Tokyo. He spins his top, which topples, to prove to himself that he is indeed out of the state of a dream within a dream and is now in the real world. The scene then proceeds with a real-time conversation with his children on the phone. After all the stress of conducting the complex process of extraction for Saito and his eventual escape, he clearly needs contact with the children he loves and to whom he longs to return. Whether his work be morally reprehensible or not then, Cobb is seen again as a man whose prime concern is for his children. His relationship to his chidren is not uncomplicated, however. His son James has clearly not accepted that his mother will never return: 'Is Mommy with you?' And Cobb tries, obviously not for the first time, to help him accept the truth of Mal's death: 'James, we talked about this. Mommy's not here anymore.' When Arthur comes to tell him that the helicopter has arrived, we learn also that he has some regret for allowing his personal problems to threaten the success of the extraction operation: Cobb apologises to Arthur for the disturbance caused by Mal.

While Cobb was sitting in the room where he had the phone conversation, the audience had been shown Cobb's gun on the table in front of him. This indicates clearly that occasions must arise in his work when he fis in danger of physical harm. It prompts the viewer to wonder how responsibly he will act when occasions arise on which it might be required. When Cobb and Arthur reach the helicopter on the roof, such an occasion occurs, throwing further light on Cobb's moral values. As they reach the door of the helicopter, it slides open, to reveal Saito and, on the far side of him, Nash, the other collaborator of Cobb, covered in blood. Nash, it appears, had tried to strike a bargain for his life with Saito. Saito gives Cobb the chance of punishing Nash for his betrayal and offers him a gun. Cobb then demonstrates that although he may undertake unethical tasks, he is no revengeful gangster: 'That's not the way I deal with things.' Saito also does not have Nash killed but decides to leave him to his fate at the hands of Cobol Engineering. This sequence is thus important for establishing some sympathy in the audience with both Cobb and Saito.

When Saito askes Cobb to perform inception, planting an idea in the mind of one of his chief rivals, Cobb at first refuses, but then Saito tempts him with an offer which it is difficult for him to refuse: 'How would you like to go home? To America. To your chidren?' Saito's own motivation clearly arises from the need to protect his own business interests: 'My main competitor is an old man in poor health. His son will soon inherit control of the corporation. I need him to decide to break up his father's empire.' Saito cannot actually guarantee what he promises Cobb as his reward, but he assures him that he is capable of fulfilling his promise. With the faintest of nods Cobb shows that he agrees to Saito's conditions. Their agreement thus becomes not just one for mutual benefit but also one of mutual trust, which also explains why Cobb is willing to take the risk later of returning to Limbo to save Saito.

In the scene in which Cobb talks with his father-in-law, Miles, in a lecture hall of the École d'Architecture in Paris, there are a few hints only of how Cobb came to his present occupation. It becomes clear from the conversation that Cobb learned the technique he employs for the purposes of extraction, and indeed inception, from Miles. Cobb says to him: 'I'm just doing what I know. I'm doing what you taught me.' But it is also clear that Miles had not intended the procedure to be used for illegal ends: 'I never taught you to be a thief.' Cobb's defence is that to ensure his own survival he had no other option. But still we do not know what he has done to make him a fugitive from American justice. He thus accepts that what he is doing is morally wrong but feels also that he had no choice in the matter: '...after what happened there weren't a whole lot of legitimate ways for me to use that skill.' He explains to Miles that for the job he has been offered he needs a skillful architect, and when Miles says 'Design it yourself' he replies that 'Mal won't let me'. The obsessive guilt about Mal has as powerful a hold on him as ever. There is a suggestion too that whatever it was that happened between him and Mal, he has only been able to live since then in his guilt-ridden fantasies about her. His only, tenuous link with a stable reality is through his love for his children. It is Miles' realisation of this that makes him agree to introduce him to a suitable young architect, Ariadne. When Miles begs him 'Come back to reality, Dom, please,' Cobb reassures him, and hence the audience, that the one reality he is sure of is that in which his children exist: 'Reality. Those kids, your grandchildren, waiting for their father to come home. That's their reality.'

Ariadne is not given a completely free hand by Cobb in her designs. His initial test of her requiring her to draw complex and difficult mazes is to ensure that his architect can design structures which disturbances from his own unconscious (i.e. Mal) could not easily penetrate, thus allowing him time to escape and defend himself.

During the sequence when Cobb is walking with Ariadne through her recreation of Paris streets and explaining the nature of dreams to her, they come to a bridge, which he suddenly recognises. It clearly has associations for him with Mal, and this evokes a memory of her, which appears in the film as an image of her smiling and laughing, with her hair blowing. He warns Ariadne against doing what he has clearly been doing himself (Arthur comments to Ariadne later that Cobb often does what he tells others not to do): 'Never recreate places from your memory. Always imagine new places.' He tells her the reason for this: 'Because building a dream from your own memories is the easiest way to lose your grasp on what's real and what's a dream.' We learn later, of course, that this is precisely what happened to Mal and it is also the reason why Cobb feels that he can only really live in his dreams. Although he clearly seems to be alluding to his own experience, he is not ready to admit it at this stage. Essentially he is repressing the truth about himself. When Ariadne asks 'Is that what happened to you?' he denies it: 'This has nothing to do with me, understand?' She is getting far too close to the truth for comfort, which is why his projections of passers-by become very aggressive towards Ariadne, and eventually his projection of Mal reappears at her most aggressive: she strides towards Ariadne, and Ariadne screams to Cobb to wake her up, as Mal lunges at her with a large knife.

When Yusuf shows Cobb and Eames a room full of men experiencing a shared dream, we learn a little more about the likely state of Mal's mind before she killed herself. Eames expresses wonderment at the fact that the men come there every day to sleep. An old man, who seems to be supervising the dreamers, contradicts him: 'No... They come here to be woken up... the dream has become their reality.' The old man also seems to have some mysterious sense that Cobb especially understands what he means. He turns to Cobb and says: 'Who are you to say otherwise, sir?' Then, when Cobb tests the drug on himself, he has a particularly vivid memory, a dream image of Mal, in which she challenges him to join her, to kill himself so that he would, she believes, leave his 'dreamworld' and join her in 'reality'. The train imagery is clearly associated with such a suicide attempt here. There is a close-up of a railway line with the sound of an approaching train. Cobb and Mal are lying with their faces against one of the rails. Mal says to him 'You know how to find me. You know what you have to do.'

There is a scene in Mombasa which is important for establishing moral justification for the task of inception which the team has agreed to undertake, and, as Cobb is the team's leader, it reinforces his moral status. Members of the team are discussing the challenges they face in the execution of their plan. Saito is reluctant at first to explain why he needs them to carry out inception on Robert Fischer, heir to the Fischer Morrow energy conglomerate, but Cobb reminds him of the seriousness of the enterprise. They will essentially be changing a man's whole personality:

> This isn't your typical corporate espionage. You asked me for inception. I do hope you understand the gravity of that request. Now the seed that we plant in this man's mind will grow into an idea. This idea will define him. It may come to change... Well, it may come to change everything about him.

This clearly demonstrates that Cobb is very much aware of the moral responsibility entailed in the enterprise. The scene also presents Saito's motivation in a more favourable light, and one which Cobb can accept. Though Saito may be concerned to protect the interests of his own company against his 'main competitor', he is also aware that if they do not break up the Fischer empire, then it will exert enormous power throughout the world due to its monopoly status. In Saito's words:

> We're the last company standing between them and total energy dominance and we can no longer compete. In effect they become a new superpower. The world needs Robert Fischer to change his mind.

In the scene in which Ariadne finds Cobb in the workshop unpacking the mechanism case, she seems to sense that his obsession with Mal is becoming more intense, and therefore might pose a serious threat to the success of their enterprise: 'You've got to warn them if it's getting worse.' And now Cobb admits to her the reason why he cannot go home, why he is forever 'on the run': 'Because they think I killed her.'

Clearly Cobb is torn between trying to rid himself of his guilt about the past and his wish to continue to be with Mal. He self-consciously allows himself to indulge in an illusion that he and Mal are still together, and indeed also with the children. There is evidence for this in the sequence in which Ariadne comes upon him in the workshop already plugged into the machine and decides to join him in his dream. She observes Cobb and Mal secretly while they are talking together. Mal is reminding Cobb of when he asked her to marry her. At that time Cobb expressed the wish 'that we'd grow old together'. Suddenly Cobb becomes aware of Ariadne's presence and he goes to the lift by which Ariadne has arrived and hits the button for the top floor. But they stop at a level which is clearly a wish-fulfillment of Cobb's: there is a beach scene which is reminiscent of the one in the opening of the film: two children are crouched down building a sandcastle. The difference is that in this later scene Mal is sitting beside them. Cobb tells Ariadne something of which we had a hint in the scene when he first encountered Yusuf and in the room with the sleeping men: 'This is the only way I can still dream.' That is to say that only artificially induced dreams are possible for him now. It is thus important for him because it gives him the illusion of being together as a family again: 'In my dreams... we're still together.'

Ariadne then accuses Cobb of doing precisely what he told her not to do: 'These aren't just dreams. These are memories. And you said never to use memories.' She interprets what he is doing as an indication that he cannot let go of his relationship with Mal: 'You're trying to keep her alive. You can't let her go.' But he insists that she does not understand what it is that he is doing and why he is doing it: 'These are moments I regret. They're memories that I have to change.' This emphasises painfully the irony of the recurrent refrain from the Edith Piaf song which features so frequently in the film: 'je ne regrette rien' ('I regret nothing'). In a sense then he is attempting inception on himself, trying to alter his own memories. Why would he want to do that? The answer must be so that he would then no longer need to feel guilty about them. He can, after all, no longer change the actual events that occurred in the past.

Ariadne clearly wants to return to the basement to find out the truth: 'Well, what's down there that you regret?' But Cobb takes her to the third floor, to the kitchen of the house which Cobb identifies as that belonging to him and Mal. They see his children playing in the garden. It is a recurring dream for Cobb. He wants to see their faces one last time, but every time in the dream he realises he has left it too late: 'And whatever I do, I can't change this moment. As I'm about to call out to them... they run away.' While he has been preoccupied with his own thoughts Ariadne has gone to the lift again and slammed the door. She presses the button again to make the lift descend. She encounters Mal and both she and the audience learn about the depth of the relationship that has existed between Mal and Cobb. It was fully interdependent. Mal asks Ariadne: 'Do you know what it is to be a lover? To be half of a whole?' And we learn more about the the train metaphor. For both of them, it had meant commitment:

> I'll tell you a riddle. You're waiting for a train. A train that will take you far away. You know where you hope this train will take you, but you don't know for sure... But... *it doesn't matter*. How can it not matter to you where the train will take you? (The italics are in the shooting script, p.110)

Cobb has appeared and answers the question she has posed: 'Because you'll be together.' It is what he had promised her and what she as his own projection is now reproaching him with. When Cobb escapes with Ariadne back into the lift and shuts the heavy grid-like gate against Mal, this clearly indicates, in terms of dream symbolism, Cobb's attempt to shut out again from his mind thoughts of what he promised Mal and how he failed her. He is not yet ready to break the hold the memory of Mal has over him. He says to her 'Please, I need you to stay here just for now.' And a little later, still tied to the memory by a wish to recover the love he has lost, he adds 'I'll come back for you, I promise.'

Shortly after the beginning of the actual inception process and within the first level of the dream, the team are in the warehouse. At one point Yusuf reveals that he had agreed to go along with the plan because Cobb said that he had carried out inception before and because he had offered Yusuf his whole share of the payment due to him. This is significant in that it emphasises yet again that Cobb is truly not in it for the money. As he reminds Arthur, 'I did what I had to to get back to my children.'

In a conversation between Cobb and Ariadne she reminds him that the rest of the team do not know the truth about him that she knows. In words, which have already been quoted in another context, she refers to:

> The truth that at any minute you might bring a freight train through the wall. The truth that Mal is bursting up through your subconscious. The truth that as we go deeper into Fischer, we're also going deeper into your subconscious – and I'm not sure we're going to like what we find.

He decides to reveal more details to her of how he experimented on accessing dreams with Mal, which essentially involved going on a reckless adventure into the subconscious mind, not understanding the risks they were taking:

> We were working together. We were exploring the concept of a dream within a dream. I kept pushing things. I wanted to go deeper and deeper. I wanted to go further. I just did not understand the concept that hours could turn into years down there, that we could get trapped so deep that when we wound up on the shore of our own subconscious… we lost sight of what was real.

It is thus clear that Cobb's sense of guilt and responsibility for Mal's death is not due to having conducted a cold-hearted experiment but is rooted in his recklessness and failure to act responsibly at the time.

Cobb tells Ariadne that he and Mall stayed in the world they created for 'something like 50 years'. At first they enjoyed 'feeling like gods', but eventually the fatal difference between his and Mal's feelings about their world became only to clear. He could never forget the unreality of it all: 'The problem was knowing that none of it was real. Eventually it just became impossible fro me to live like that.' But Mal, on the other hand, had managed to accept the world they had created as real. He uses the metaphor of locking something away again: 'She had locked something away, something deep inside her, a truth that she had once known but chose to forget.' We see Mal in her childhood home with a doll's house, inside which is a safe. Mal is seen putting a spinning top inside it and locking it again. In other words she shuts out of her consciousness the one method of distinguishing between what is real and what is unreal. In voice-over Cobb says 'Limbo became her reality.'

When Cobb and Mal eventually wake up again into the 'real world', Cobb is able to adapt, but Mal cannot. She believed that the real world was not in fact real and that

The spinning top, now still

they needed to wake up again to get back to the true 'real world'. This is the root of his sense of guilt: he had brought about the state of mind in Mal in which she believed 'that in order to get back home we had to kill ourselves'. She also believed that their children were only projections and 'that our *real* children were waiting for us up there..

Cobb then explains to Ariadne how Mal's death eventually came about, how she sat out on the ledge of the window of the hotel suite opposite theirs, dangling her feet over empty space below. Before Mal jumps to her death she attempts to blackmail him into joining her, telling him 'I filed a letter with our attorney, explaining how I'm fearful for my safety, how you've threatened to kill me.' Ariadne reveals herself to be a perceptive psychologist: 'Your guilt defines her. It's what powers her.' In other words, until he manages to get over his sense of guilt about her death, her image will continue to haunt him and disrupt his endeavours. He must learn to accept that she was responsible for her own decisions: 'But you are not responsible for the idea that destroyed her.' For the obsession to cease, and to prevent it from sabotaging their project, he must do two things: '...you have to forgive yourself, and you're gonna have to confront her.' These are the two key principles that Cobb must follow if he is to find redemption.

Later, in the hotel lobby sequence, something occurs which seems to indicate that Cobb is indeed becoming firmer and more resolute in dealing with his own disruptive projections: as he is escorting Fischer out of the lobby he catches a glimpse of the backs of his two children, another disturbance from his own subconscious, but this time he resolutely ignores them.

While he appears to be more resolute he is still not completely immune to intrusions from his subconscious. There is a hint of this when the team prepare to enter the third level dream, set in the snow-covered mountains. As Cobb starts falling asleep under the influence of the drug, we see a brief image of billowing white curtains like those in the hotel suite where Cobb and Mal stayed, clearly an intimation of the disruptive threat that still lurks in Cobb's subconscious.

As the subsecurity has become more aggressive in this final level of dreaming (Eames had just warned them that it would be so), so also has Cobb's projection of Mal. The team are getting near to their goal, so that the Fischer's subsecurity is becoming more determined to destroy the intruders. And Mal, the embodiment of the disruptive force of Cobb's guilt complex, is also becoming more lethal in her attempts to thwart Cobb's project.

When Cobb and Ariadne are inside the fortified hospital, Cobb becomes suddenly aware that he has Mal in the sights of his weapon. Ariadne causes some indecision in Cobb's mind by reminding him that they must focus on Fischer. She reminds him that the image of Mal he is looking at is not real, but that 'Fischer, Fischer is real'. Before Cobb can decide what to do, Mal has shot Fischer, and then Cobb shoots Mal. This all happens very quickly, and the moment of killing Mal passes without much emphasis in the film. It soon becomes clear, however, that Cobb's struggle with his projection of Mal is just shifting to another level, the ultimate level in the film: limbo.

Fischer is mortally wounded, and despite Eames' attempts to revive him with a conveniently placed defibrillator Cobb is ready to give up: 'It won't do any good. There's no use reviving him. His mind's already trapped down there. It's all over.' But Ariadne manages to persuade the others that they can follow Fischer down to limbo and bring him back up when the 'kick' occurs. Her only concern is that Cobb may not be able to deal with Mal when he encounters her 'down there'. But Cobb feels he will be able to cope with the situation. He can guess the way in which Mal's mind will have been working. She will have Fischer nearby: 'She wants me to come after him. She wants me back down there with her.' This suggests that, as Mal is Cobb's projection, there is a part of him which still wants to be with Mal, but that he is determined to fight against it.

Once they are in limbo Cobb shows Ariadne around the world that he and Mal had created together. There is a moment when it seems that his love for his children might deflect him from his goal. In a side street he notices a small boy and a girl with their back to him. He seems to resist the temptation and turns away. Cobb points out to Ariadne an important distinction between the dream world and the real world, concerning the matter of choice. It opens up a whole new philosophical perspective on the film. Talking of how he and Mal had created their world in limbo, he stresses that in the real world they would have had to live in one building at a time. In the dream world they were able to have all the houses they had lived in *at the same time*. As Cobb says to Ariadne: 'We both wanted to live in a house, but we both loved this type of building, skyscrapers. In the real world we'd have to choose, but not here.'

They come across Mal seated in a kitchen and she tries to unsettle Ariadne by throwing doubt on Cobb's own sense of what is and is not real. As a projection of his own subconscious, Mal thus reveals Cobb's self-doubts. Is not what he considers real also dreamlike?

No creeping doubts? Not feeling persecuted, Dom? Chased around the globe by anonymous corporations and police forces? The way the projections pursue the dreamer?

Mal reminds Cobb that he does have freedom of choice in the matter. He can choose one reality or the other: 'Choose to be here. Choose me.' She continues to throw doubt on his belief that he knows what is real: 'You keep telling yourself what you know... but what do you believe? What do you feel?' She is thus asking him to be irrational and to trust his intuition. In a world of uncertainty she is asking him to take a leap of faith. Cobb picks up on her use of the word 'feeling' and stresses that it is his very real feeling of guilt which convinces him that he is right (i.e. he could not feel guilt about something which he knew to be imaginary):

Guilt, I feel guilt, Mal. And no matter what I do, no matter how hopeless I am, no matter how confused, that guilt is always there, reminding me of the truth.

And the truth he is referring to is that 'the idea that caused you to question your reality came from me'.

Cobb then explains to Ariadne that he had involved his wife in an experimental trial of inception with him. His role in confusing her is represented symbolically by his continuing use of her spinning top. Cobb had found out the location of the safe in the doll's house. It was he who then made the top spin and locked it away again while it was still spinning. This represents symbolically Cobb's responsibility for making Mal convinced that the only reality was the one which she was in, and that, as she says in voice-over, 'death was the only escape'.

There follows a recapitulation of the scene we had glimpsed earlier, with some variations: Cobb and Mal are lying on a railway line and Cobb is reciting the story which Mal had told Ariadne, about the couple waiting for the train to come. This time it is Mal who completes Cobb's words with 'because you'll be together'. A train then comes and we must assume that it obliterates them. Cobb then admits, now back in limbo with Ariadne present, that he did not realise then that the idea he had placed in Mal's mind would grow, and that even when they had both come back into the real world Mal would still continue to believe that this world was not in fact real, and that death was the only escape for them.

Mal then offers to make a deal with Cobb. She is willing to let Fischer go (he is lying on the porch), if Cobb agrees to stay with her. Cobb makes it clear to Ariadne, however, that he does not intend to do such a deal with Mal, but that he needs to stay in limbo to save Saito, who is also almost dead by now. If he had been confused at times by the distinction between dreams and reality, then this confrontation with Mal has finally resolved his doubts. He is now quite sure about the difference between reality and his dream projections: 'I can't stay with her anymore because she doesn't exist.' Cobb has come at last to the point where he can clearly distinguish between Mal as a real human being and the simulacrum of her. It is this realisation which frees him from his obsession. He tries to explain to Mal that although he has created her, he was not able to recreate her perfectly: 'I can't imagine you in all your complexity and all your perfections, and all your imperfections.' Cobb then uses a word which provides a link with the myth of Hades and that of Orpheus and Euridice. He says to Mal: 'You're just a shade. You are just a *shade* of my real wife. You were the best I could do, but I'm sorry, you're just not good enough.' He has thus finally confronted Mal symbolically and is ready to turn his back on her, Orpheus-like. In one last desperate attempt Mal stabs at Cobb with a knife ('Does this feel real enough?'), but Ariadne proves to be Cobb's saviour. It is she who shoots Mal. This seems to suggest that Cobb, in his human weakness, could not bring himself to kill even the shade of the woman he loved, and he needed the outside agency of Ariadne to perform the necessary deed.

There is one more sequence with Mal which seems to suggest that Cobb learned to appreciate the value of the experience of love even though it is transient, that death does not destroy the value of shared experience. Mal says to him: 'You remember when you asked me to marry you?' Cobb confirms this. And Mal adds: 'You said you dreamed that we'd grow old together.' To this Cobb replies: 'But we did.' There is a play with the ambiguity of the word 'dreamed' here. Mal has clearly understood it in the sense of having an ideal one wishes to realise. Cobb's reply can be interpreted to mean both that 'we did grow old together' and that 'we had a dream of growing old together'. Intercut here is a shot of the hands of two elderly people clutching each other. Cobb's last words to Mal reveal that he has also finally freed himself from his obsession with her and can now move forward in his life: 'I miss you more than I can bear... but we had our time together. And I have to let you go...'

Cobb's last task is to redeem the trust put in him by Saito, and he tracks him down in the version of the Japanese castle we saw at the beginning of the film. He explains to Saito that he has come to 'to remind you of something you once knew... that this world is not real'. He asks Saito 'to take a leap of faith' and go back with him. Can it be a coincidence that the words used echo those of Mal? The difference is that the leap of faith which she required of Cobb would have resulted in his death, while Saito's will enable him to return to the real world of life.

Cobb has thus finally worked through and overcome his guilt, rid himself of his obsession with Mal, by recognising her as a shade, a poor imitation, and by honouring the trust that Saito put in him. He has also, incidentally, saved the world from domination by the Fischer Morrow Corporation!

The final ambiguous image in the film of the spinning top and Cobb's reunion with his children can therefore be interpreted as implying that maybe it does not matter whether the scene is real or not. As Cobb realised and tried to convince Mal: it is the reality of the experience which is important (see also chapter 8).

7. *Inception* and the Arts

There are specific artistic references in the film. One artist is referred to by indirect reference and visual simulation of some of his works, and another is paid homage to by the inclusion of one of his works in a scene. The artists in question are M.C. Escher and Francis Bacon.

M. C. Escher

The Dutch artist Maurits Cornelis Escher (1898-1972), famous for his works featuring constructions which would be impossible in the real world, is not directly named in the film, but he is referred to indirectly by the mention of a phenomenon which he utilised in his work: the so-called 'Penrose Steps'. This phenomenon is cited in the dialogue of the film when Arthur is explaining to Ariadne some of the geometry required to construct the architecture for the dreams. The term 'Penrose Steps' refers to an impossible staircase created by Lionel Penrose and his son Roger. They published an article about it in *The British Journal of Psychology* in 1958.[95] It seems that Escher saw the article and this resulted in his lithograph *Ascending and Descending*, first printed in March, 1960, featuring a staircase which goes back on itself and appears to form a continuous loop.

Another work of his bears even more startling resemblance to a scene in *Inception*. The lithograph *Relativity* (1953) depicts architecture in which not only do the staircases exist in different planes but also humanoid figures appear to walk between the different levels in defiance of gravity. This bears direct comparison with the sequence of shots in the film showing Arthur and Ariadne descending a similar impossible staircase. A simplified version enables Arthur to escape from and turn back on a pursuer in one of the dream states later in the film.

The Escher effect

Francis Bacon

Early on in a sequence in which Cobb is talking to Mal, there is a painting visible on the wall of the room. Mal views it and deduces that they must be in one of Arthur's dreams, as the painting reflects his taste. Cobb evasively replies that their quarry, the Japanese businessman Saito, has an interest in post-war British art. The painting is seen at quite close range and then subsequently in the background of the scene. It is not identified in the film, but in the shooting script the artist is named as Francis Bacon, though no particular work is specified. It can be identified as Bacon's *Study for a head of George Dyer*, 1967. The possible influence of this artist on the depiction of the character 'Two-Face' in Nolan's second film of the Batman trilogy has already been noted. Nolan clearly shares some perspectives on the world with Bacon: a fascination with distorted reality, a sense of horror as in a nightmare, and, in some cases, the real world being actually torn apart.

'George Dyer' and *The Dark Knight*'s Harvey Two-Face

8. The Ending: Dreams, Reality and Ambiguity

When the process of inception is completed and the team have escaped, we find ourselves back in the cabin of the 747 with all the team present. The attendant deals with the usual formalities before landing. Cobb, Arthur and Ariadne exchange smiles, and Cobb and Saito look at each other seriously. Saito takes out his mobile phone and dials. In this short scene, therefore, we are informed that all is well with the team, that both Cobb and Saito have survived, and, from his general behaviour, that Fischer does not realise what he has been through. The phone call which Saito makes, we can assume, is the one promised when they made the agreement: enabling Cobb to re-enter the USA and be together with his children again. What Saito actually says in the phone call and whom he is contacting are never made explicit. We must just assume that he has powerful contacts.

There are still some moments of tension when Cobb reaches the immigration desk. Will he be allowed through or not? But after looking Cobb up and down for a moment the official stamps his passport and says 'Welcome home, Mr. Cobb.' A suitable choice of words, although the official is of course unaware of their significance for Cobb. As the various members of the team catch sight of each other they exchange knowing glances. Fischer regards him with what one can perhaps describe as a puzzled look, as though he think he knows this man from somewhere. As Cobb emerges into the crowded arrivals area, he catches sight of Professor Miles, who is there to meet him.

That is essentially the end of the story, but the director has left us with an ambiguous ending to the film.

We next find ourselves in the home we can recognise from earlier sequences, where the children are staying. Miles and Cobb arrive, and Miles goes outside into the garden, calling the children, who are on the lawn. Meanwhile Cobb takes out his top and spins it on the table. Through the window Cobb can see the backs of the children's heads. Miles says to them: 'Look who's here!' The children turn and we, with Cobb, see their faces for the first time in the film. There is a short sequence of background dialogue inserted here, which we overhear. Whether it was improvised or not, it proves to be very apt. James says to his father, 'Look what I've been building.' Cobb is curious: 'What are you building?' And James replies, 'A house on the cliff.' Cobb says: 'On the cliff? Come on. I want you to show me.' There are other snippets of dialogue but perhaps the fact that we overhear this sequence clearly is significant: James shows signs of following in his father's footsteps! He is, in his childlike way, already interested in architecture, and we can recall perhaps the building of sandcastles in flashbacks earlier in the film. The telling detail, however, is that the boy specifies that the house is 'on the cliff'. As with the sandcastles, and as with his father, it seems that the boy is attracted by impermanence and risk!

We are then left with the challenge of the final shot of Cobb's spinning top. The image abruptly cuts to black while it is still spinning, though it does appear to wobble a little. It can be argued that the fact that it does not fall indicates that the final scene of Cobb's reunion with his children is also inside a dream. On the other hand, the fact that it wobbles suggests that it is about to fall, indicating that Cobb is indeed back in the 'real world'. Of course, the shot was designed to be deliberately ambiguous, to force the audience to look back at the film and reflect on the nature of dreams and of films and the relations of both to what we consider, often unquestioningly, to be the 'real world'.

Dream or reality?

9. Critical Reception

Rarely in the press and media is popular cinema, of which *Inception* is surely an example, subject to rigorous critical examination. Occasionally, however, some writers do provide insights worth discussing at greater depth, cues to possible lines of analysis and appraisal.

Some organisations and publications provide a quality score for a film, which indicates the strength of opinion and/or extent of its popularity. Based on reviews from 284 critics, with an average score of 8/10, the website Rotten Tomatoes awarded *Inception* a score of 86%. More worthy of consideration might be the website's comment that the film 'succeeds viscerally as well as intellectually'.[96] This could stimulate an interesting debate about the nature of the emotional content of the film, and whether this is in any way obscured by the complexity of the ideas expressed.

For those interested in further statistics, the organisation Cinemascore polled viewers during the film's opening weekend and gave it a B+ rating, i.e. 'could do better'. Metacritic analysed 42 reviews by mainstream critics and gave the film a score of 74%.[97]

Some insights by individual critics which might stimulate discussion are included below.

Positive Reviews

Justin Chang, in *Variety*, described the film as 'a heist thriller for surrealists, a Jungian Rififi'.[98] Whether this colourful description makes valid comparisons can be determined by considering the conventions of 'heist' films.

Those interested in comparing the film with other works by Nolan might like to consider Lisa Schwarzbaum's comment in *Entertainment Weekly* concerning the editing of the film: '...the backwards splicing of Nolan's own *Memento* looks rudimentary by comparison.'

See also Devin Faraci on chud.com for a discussion of whether the film is primarily about dreaming or about film-making. To what extent is it an ironical reflection on the interaction of the two? How much is it serious and how much tongue-in-cheek?

The British critic Mark Kermode has argued that the film demonstrates 'that it is possible for blockbusters and art to be the same things'.[99] In discussing this one can legitimately consider popularity and box-office statistics.

A comment by Richard Corliss in *Time* can be a starting point for discussion of the film in relation to oneiric film theory: 'The idea of moviegoing as communal dreaming [gets] a "state-of-the-art" update with *Inception*.'[100]

Kenneth Turan, in *The Los Angeles Times*, praised Nolan for his trying to blend 'the best of traditional and modern filmmaking'.[101] Which raises the question, what traditional techniques does Nolan use and which aspects are innovative?

Negative Reviews

Many negative reviews of the film are simply dismissive and lacking in any justification, but here and there one can find some provocative statements worthy of serious consideration. An example is the comment by A. O. Scott in *The New York Times*: '…there is nothing that counts as genuine vision. Mr. Nolan's idea of the mind is too literal, too logical, and too rule-bound to allow the full measure of madness.'[102] This is an evaluation that must be taken seriously. In the light of contemporary theories about the nature of mind and consciousness, the notion of inception can be seriously challenged.[103]

And is the film perhaps too clever and intricate for its own good? Has the puzzle of Chinese boxes finally obscured the treatment of the main ideas in the film? On this issue David Denby, in *The New Yorker*, has commented: '*Inception* is a stunning-looking film that gets lost in fabulous intricacies, a movie devoted to its own workings and to little else.'[104]

One critic has commented that the film '…closely resembles the structure of a video-game. It sets up a world where narrative is reversible and several things can go on at the same time, at different speeds.'[105] Keen videogamers might like to consider how far they would go along with this judgement. This review appeared in *The Guardian*, online edition. There are other negative reviews in the same publication, which are worth reading: by Philip French (18 July, 2010) and by David Cox (20 July, 2010). Anthony Quinn, in *Independent.com*, has argued that however technically brilliant the film may be, it is let down by a poor storyline: 'how to dupe the unloved son of a tycoon into breaking up his business empire.'[106] And in the same edition of this newspaper Jonathan Romney provides perhaps the most scathing judgement on the film: 'Dream, as seen here, is controlled, designed, pre-programmed, policed. *Inception* is not a hymn to the imagination so much as a militant oppression of it – a film that reduces dream to the mundane logic of the action movie.'[107]

10. Further Lines of Inquiry

Cutting and Point of View

Christopher Nolan has said that he cannot cut a film without considering whose point of view the shot represents: 'Whether in the pure camera blocking or even the writing, it's all about point of view. I can't cut a scene if I haven't already figured out whose point of view I'm looking at, and I can't shoot the scene in a neutral way.'[108] He cites as an example: 'Stylistically, something that runs through my films is the shot that walks into a room behind a character, because to me, that takes me inside the way that character enters.'[109] He says that he has found that what he calls 'more objective camera techniques' do not work for him in this respect.[110] Such techniques are, for example, 'a longer lens, flattening things out, using multi-camera'.[111] He also does not like to use zoom lenses: 'I don't reframe using the zoom. Instead, we always move the camera physically closer and put a different focal length on.'[112]

Students might care to discuss the camerawork in *Inception* taking into account Nolan's preferences and analyse specific scenes which exemplify them. Is he always true to these principles? And do they have drawbacks?

The Music

The Piaf Song

At various points in this book attention has been drawn to the role in the film of the song 'Non, je ne regrette rien', in the original recording by Édith Piaff. As well as serving functionally as a musical cue to the dreamers of the imminence of the 'kick', which will take them out of their dream state and back to the real world, it also supplies an ironical comment on Cobb's personal situation.

For copyright reasons it is not possible to quote the whole song here, but its general tenor is the determination to shut out the past, shake off both good and bad memories, and to regret nothing that one has done, but to start a new life with a new relationship. The irony is, of course, that Cobb cannot shut out the past, his memories of Mal, and that he clearly regrets very much what he has done. Only after a thorough process of catharsis can he return to his children and start a new life.

We cannot hear the whole song in detail in the film, but we do hear frequently the opening refrain:

Non, rien de rien,

Non. Je ne regrette rien.

There are many translations of the whole song on the internet, but most are inaccurate in some details. The only accurate and idiomatic translation I could find was by Shava Nerad:

No, nothing at all,

I regret nothing.[113]

The second verse ends:

C'est payé, balayé, oublié.

Je me fous du passé!

Which is rendered as:

It's bought and paid for, wiped away, forgotten,

I don't give a damn about the past.[114]

The song ends with the words:

Car ma vie, car mes joies

Aujourd'hui, ça commence avec toi.

This is rendered as:

Because my life, because my joys

Today, I begin with you.[115]

Hans Zimmer's score

In his article, Todd Martens reports on an interview with Hans Zimmer and Johnny Marr, who were responsible for the film's score, in which Martens quotes Zimmer as saying that, for him, 'the soul of the film' can be traced to the Piaf song.[116] In Zimmer's words: 'What I was writing was nostalgia and sadness. This character [Cobb] carries this sadness all the time that he cannot express... I think the job that Johnny and I had to do was write *the heart* of this thing.'[117] And he adds later that 'underneath is a story about a person who is in utter torment'.[118] According to Martens, 'Pieces of Piaf's interpretation of the song were stretched, manipulated and woven into Zimmer's score.'[119]

Marketing

The film's official website,[120] set up before the release of the film, features amongst other things, an animation of Cobb's spinning top, an online game called *Mind Game*, and an online manual of the PASIV device, the mechanism in the metal box, which makes the inception process possible.

It is worth considering whether these are effective means of advertising the film and awakening interest in it? Do they give away too much?

Mythological Aspects

There are several mythological references in the film, and it is worth examining whether they broaden the films frames of reference in any way.

Ariadne and the Labyrinth

The most explicit mythological reference is to Ariadne and the labyrinth. The terms labyrinth and maze are often used interchangeably. In common parlance they both imply a complex branching puzzle, with choices of path and direction (some labyrinths are unicursal with a single non-branching path). In Greek mythology,

Ariadne was the daughter of King Minos of Crete. At the centre of the famous labyrinth in Crete was the Minotaur, part-man and part-bull, to which sacrificial victims were fed. Theseus, the son of King Aegeus, volunteered to kill the Minotaur. Ariadne fell in love with him and gave him a sword and a ball of thread so that he could find his way out of the labyrinth after performing the deed. In *Inception* Ariadne becomes the person to accompany Cobb and protect him against the destructive force of Mal and to help him escape afterwards.

Orpheus and Euridice

Parallels can also be drawn with the myth of Orpheus and Euridice. Orpheus was allowed to bring his dead wife Euridice back from the Underworld to the world of the living, provided the he did not look back at her while doing so. The motif of 'not looking back' is transposed to Cobb's relationship with his children in the film: he avoids seeing their faces until he can meet them again in the real world. And in the film Cobb finally accepts that his projection of Mal is not like the real Mal in all her complexity but just a shade, and he lets her go.

Limbo

The limbo of the film is described as 'unstructured dream space', where the protagonists could become trapped forever. Historically the term is closely associated with mythological aspects of the Catholic church. The word comes from the Latin 'limbus', meaning an edge or boundary and more specifically implying the edge of Hell. It is an area of the afterlife to which those people are assigned who die in original sin, but who are not condemned to the Hell of the Damned. In colloquial speech, holding something 'in limbo' means that its progress is held up until something happens to change the circumstances. The concept of limbo in the film is thus unique to the imagined process of inception.

Notes

1. 'The Man behind the Mask' www.ucl.ac.uk/display/SLAISFAlumni/Christopher+Nolan 8 December, 2008.
2. 'The Making of Following' by Johannes Duncker. www.christophernolan.net
3. www.medical-dictionary.thefreedictionary.com
4. Adapted Screenplay,' by David S. Cohen, Variety, 18 December, 2006.
5. Jung, C.G., *The Collected Works of C. G. Jung*, vol. 9, p. I, para . 221, Routledge and Kegan Paul Ltd., UK, 1953-1978.
   Man and His Symbols, (ed. C.G. Jung), Part 1, 'Approaching the Unconscious,' written by C.G. Jung, Dell Publications (1964) 1968, p.38.
6. ibid.
7. Jung, C.G., *Psychological Types, in The Collected Works of C.G. Jung*, vol 8, 'The Structure and Dynamics of the Psyche, Routledge and Kegan Paul Ltd., UK, (1960) 1969, p. 246.
8. James, David (January 14, 2008). 'Indy, Batman, Narnia All Return in 2008' (www.msnbc.msn.com/id22653902).
9. www.guardian.co.uk/film/filmblog/2012/jul/17/dark-knight-rises-capitalist-superhero
10. www.rollingstone.com/movies/news/christopher-nolan-dark-knight-rises-isn-t-political-20120720
11. Jolin, Dan (November 2014). 'The Ultimate Trip'. In *Empire* (www.empireonline.com/news/story.asp).
12. Itzkoff, Dave, 'A Man and His Dream: Christopher Nolan and *Inception*,' artsbeat.blogs.nytimes.com/2010/06/30/a-man-and-his-dream-christopher-nolan-and-inception
13. Weintraub, Steve, 'Christopher Nolan and Emma Thomas Interview,' www.collider.com/2010/03/25/director-christopher-nolan-and-producer-emma-yhomas-interview-inception
14. Dan, John, 'Crime of the Century,' June 30, 2010, *Empire*, pp. 93-94.
15. www.warnerbros.co.uk/inception/mainsite/pdf/INCEPTION_PK_Notes, p.3.
16. Weintraub, Steve, see note 2.
17. ibid. p.4.
18. ibid.
19. www.warnerbros.co.uk/inception/mainsite/pdf/INCEPTION_PK_Notes p.5.
20. ibid.
21. ibid.
22. ibid. p.6.
23. ibid. p.12.
24. Weintraub, Steve, see note 2.
25. http://theplaylist.blogspot.com/2010/06/13/christopher-nolan-tested-3d-conversion.html

26. www.latimes.com/business/la-ct-inception-20100713,0,319222story

27. Owen, Matt, http.//econsultancy.com/us/blog/6277-inception-multichannel-marketing-that-works-like-a-dream

28. Hiscock, John (july 1, 2010), www.telegraph.co.uk/culture/films/filmmakersonfilm/78666 77/7Christopher-Nolan-interview.html

29. Boucher, Geoff (April 4, 2010), www.latimes.com/entertainemnet/news/la-ca-inception4-2010apr04,6869939.story

30. ibid.

31. www.collider.com/2010/03/25/director-christopher-nolan-and-producer-emma-thomas-interview-inception

32. ibid.

33. Marikar, Sheila (July 16, 2010), 'Inside Inception,' abcnews.go.com/Entertainment/inside-inception-christopher-nolans-dream-world-exist-real/story

34. Itzkoff, Dave (June 30, 2010), artsbeat.blogs,nytimes.com/2010/o6/30/a-man-and-his-dream—christopher-nolan-and-inception/

35. Itzkoff, Dave (June 30, 2010),www.nytimes.com/2010/07/04/movies/04inception.html

36. Meehan, Paul, *Tech-Noir, The Fusion of Science Fiction and Film Noir*, Mcfarland and co. inc., Jefferson, North Carolina, and London, 2008, p.17.

37. ibid. p.13.

38. Lee, Daryl, *The Heist Film, Stealing with Style*, Mayflower, London and New York, 2014, chapters 1 and 2.

39. See 'Production Notes,' page 9: www.warnerbros.co.uk/inception/mainsite/pdf/INCEPTION_PK_Notes

40. Jameson, Richard T., (ed), *They Went Thataway: Redefining Film Genres, A National Society of Film Critics Guide*, San Francisco, Mercury House, 1994, p.ix.

41. Altman, Rick, 'A semantic/syntactic approach to film genre,' *Cinema Journal* 23, no 3 (Spring 1984), pp. 6-18.

42. Altman, Rick, *Film/Genre*, BFI, 1999, p.207.

43. ibid.

44. Altman, 1999, p.214.

45. Altman, 1999. P.219 (Note: the 1984 article is included in an appendix to the 1999 book, pages 216-225, and this and subsequent references are to its location there).

46. ibid.

47. ibid.

48. Altman, 1999, p.220.

49. ibid. p. 221.

50. ibid. p. 221-222.

51. ibid. p. 222.

52. ibid. p. 225.
53. Lee, Daryl, *The Heist Film, Stealing with Style*, Wallflower, London and New York, 2014, p.93.
54. Kaminsky, Stuart M., *American Film Genres: Approaches to a Critical Theory of Popular Film*, Dayton Ohio, 1974.p.79. Cited in Lee, Daryl, 2014, p.5.
55. Lee, Daryl, 2014, p.98.
56. ibid.
57. All three phrases from Lee, Daryl, 2014, p.99.
58. Scalzi, 2005, p.38.
59. Scalzi, 2005, p.39.
60. Scalzi, 2005, p.40.
61. Scalzi, 2005, p.45.
62. Scalzi, 2005, p.46.
63. Means, Loren, 'Science Fiction – The Last ten Years,' YLEM Journal, number 2, vol.23, Jan-Feb 2003, p.2.
64. ibid.
65. Meehan, Paul, *Tech Noir, The Fusion of Science Fiction and Film Noir*, McFarland and Co. Inc., Jefferson, North Carolina, and London, 2008, p.1.
66. ibid. p.2.
67. ibid. p.16.
68. Oxford English Dictionary.
69. *The Interpretation of Dreams* [1900], Sigmund Freud, The Penguin Freud Library, vol.4. Penguin, (1976)1991, p.453.
70. *Dreaming*, Oxford University Press, New York, USA, 2002, republished in the 'Very Short Introduction' series, Oxford, UK, 2005.
71. *General Aspects of Dream Psychology* (1948). C. G. Jung, The Collected Works of C. G. Jung, vol 8, 'The Structure and Dynamics of the Psyche,' Routledge and Kegan Paul Ltd., UK (1960), 1969, p.264.
72. ibid. p.266.
73. ibid.
74. *Introductory Lectures on Psychoanalysis* [1916-1917], Sigmund Freud, The Pelican Freud Library, vol.1. Penguin, 1973, p.205.
75. ibid.
76. ibid. p.208.
77. ibid. p.209.
78. ibid.
79. ibid.
80. ibid. p.183.

81. ibid. p.185.

82. *Man and His Symbols*, (ed. C.G. Jung), Part 1, 'Approaching the Unconscious,' written by C. G. Jung, Dell Publications, (1964) 1968, p.17.

83. ibid. p.37.

84. ibid. p.41.

85. *General Aspects of Dream Psychology* (1948), C. G. Jung, The Collected Works of C.G. Jung, vol 8, 'The Structure and Dynamics of the Psyche,' Routledge and Kegan Paul Ltd., UK (1960) 1969, p. 246.

86. *Man and His Symbols*, (ed. C. G. Jung), Part 1, 'Approaching the Unconscious,' written by C. G. Jung, Dell Publications (1964) 1968, p.38.

87. ibid. p.56.

88. *Man and His Symbols*, (ed. C. G. Jung), Part 1, 'Approaching the Unconscious,' written by C. G. Jung, Dell Publications (1964), 1968, p.57.

89. ibid.

90. *Psychological Types* (1921), C. G. Jung, The Collected Works of C.G. Jung, vol. 6, Routledge and Kegan Paul Ltd, UK, 1971, p. 400.

91. ibid. p.443.

92. *Man and His Symbols*, (ed. C. G Jung), Part 1, 'Approaching the Unconsscious,' written by C. G. Jung, Dell Publications (1964), 1968,p.67.

93. ibid. p.87.

94. ibid.

95. Penrose and Penrose, BJP, 1958, pp.31-33.

96. www.rottentomatoes.com/movie/inception

97. Stewart, Andrew, (July 18, 2010) 'Inception tops weekend box office.' www.variety.com/article/VR1118021880.html

98. Chang, Justin, 'Inception' (July 5, 2010), www.variety.com/review

99. Kermode, Mark (December 24, 2010) *Kermode Uncut: My Top Five Films of the Year*, www.bbc.co.uk/markkermode/2010/12

100. Corliss, Richard (July 14, 2010), '*Inception*: Whose Mind Is It Anyway?' www.time./arts/article/

101. Turan, Kenneth (July 16,2010). www.latimes.com/entertainment/news/la-et-inception

102. Scott, A. O., (July 15, 2010), 'This Time the Dream's on Me,' www.movies.nytimes.com/2010/07/16/movies/169inception.html

103. For a stimulating survey of current theories, see Blackmore, Susan, *Consciousness*, OUP, 2005.

104. Denby, David (July 26, 2010), 'Dream Factory' www.newyorker.com/magazine/2010/07/26/dream-factory

105. Thorpe, Vanessa (July 25, 2010), 'How Inception Proves the Art of Baffling Films Does Make Sense,' https://www.theguardian.com/film/2010/jul/25/inception-christopher-nolan-leonardo-dicaprio

106. Quinn, Anthony (Friday July 18, 2010) www.independent.com

107. Romney, Jonathan (Friday July 18, 2010) www.independent.com

108. Ressner, Jeffery (Spring 2012), 'The Traditionalist,' DGA Quarterly (www.dga.org/Craft/DGAQ/All-Articles).

109. ibid.

110. ibid.

111. ibid.

112. ibid.

113. http://lyricstranslate.com/en/non-je-regrette-rien-no-i-regret-nothing

114. ibid.

115. ibid.

116. http://herocomplex.latimes.com/movies/inception-christopher-nolan-the-smiths-johnny-marr

117. ibid.

118. ibid.

119. ibid.

120. www.inceptionmovie.com

General Bibliography

Primary sources are identified in the Notes. The following are works recommended for further reading on specific topics.

Script

Nolan, Christopher, *Inception, The Shooting Script*, Insight Editions, USA, 2010.

On genre

Altman, Rick, *Film/Genre*, BFI, UK, 1999.

Jameson, Richard T. (ed.), *They Went Thataway: Redefining Film Genres*, A National Society of Film Critics Guide, Mercury House, San Francisco, 1994.

On the heist genre

Lee, Daryl, *The Heist Film, Stealing with Style*, Columbia University Press, 2014.

On science fiction film

Bould, Mark, 'Film and Television,' ch.5 of: James, Edward and Mendlesohn, Farah (eds), *The Cambridge Companion to Science Fiction*, CUP, 2003.

Hanson, Matt, *Building Sci-fi Moveiscapes, The Science Behind the Fiction*, Page One, Singapore, 2005.

Perkowitz, Sidney, *Hollywood Science, Movies, Science, and the End of the World*, Columbia Press, New York, 2007.

Scalzi, John, *The Rough Guide to Sci-fi Movies*, Penguin, UK, 2005.

Seed, David, *Science Fiction*, Oxford University Press, 2011.

On tech-noir

Augur, Emily E., *Tech-Noir Film, A Theory of the Development of Popular Genres*, Intellect, Bristol, UK and Chicago, USA, 2011.

Meehan, Paul, *Tech-Noir, The Fusion of Science Fiction and Film Noir*, McFarland and Company, Inc., Jefferson, North Carolina and London, 2008.

On dream theory and the mind

Blackmore, Susan, *Consciousness*, Oxford University Press, 2005.

Freud, Sigmund, *Introductory Lectures on Psychoanalysis* (1916-1917), The Pelican Freud Library, vol 1., Penguin, 1973.

Freud, Sigmund, *The Interpretation of Dreams* (1900), The Pelican Freud Library, vol 4., Penguin, 1976.

Hobson, J. Allan, *Dreaming*, Oxford University Press, 2003.

Jung, C. G. (ed.), *Man and His Symbols*, Dell Publications, (1964), 1968.